PAYING TOO MUCH

TAX

Be Empowered,

Library and Archives Canada Cataloguing in Publication

DeRooy-Pearson, Marilyn, 1957-, author
    Paying too much tax : a business owner's guide to
corporate structures and saving tax / Marilyn deRooy-Pearson.

Issued in print and electronic formats.
ISBN 978-1-77141-116-5 (pbk.).--ISBN 978-1-77141-117-2
(html)

    1. Family-owned business enterprises--Canada. 2.
Family-owned
business enterprises--Taxation--Canada. 3. Tax planning--Canada.
I. Title.

KE1450 D47 2015   346.71'0668   C2015-901230-9
KF1380 D47 2015

                                              C2015-901231-7

PAYING TOO MUCH
TAX

A business owner's guide to

corporate structures and saving tax

Marilyn deRooy-Pearson

First Published in Canada 2015 by Influence Publishing

Cover Designer: Trista Baldwin
Portrait and Cover Photographer: Randal Kurt Photography
Senior Editor: Sue Kehoe
Assistant Editor: Nina Shoroplova
Production Editor: Jennifer Kaleta
Typeset: Greg Salisbury

DISCLAIMER: This book is for information purposes only and should not be construed as legal or tax advice. Every effort has been made to ensure its accuracy, but errors and omissions are possible.

All comments related to taxation are general in nature and are based on 2014 Canadian tax legislation for Canadian residents, which is subject to change. Persons who are not residents of Canada or those who are resident in Canada but are citizens of another country may be subject to different tax rules. They may also be subject to taxes levied by jurisdictions other than Canada. In addition, this book contemplates the application of tax laws in common law provinces and, therefore, not in the Province of Quebec.

Once more, the Parke family story and the characters named in this book are fictitious. They are a compilation of stories from the many businesses my company and I have helped with tax planning over the years.

The tax-related information contained in this book is current as of December 31, 2014.

This book is dedicated to my amazing children, Vanessa and Zach. You are my pride and joy! You are my inspiration! Your love has given me the strength to be the best that I can be.

Testimonials

"This book is amazing! I work in the financial industry and it wasn't until I read this book that the whole financial planning process came together for me. And I have read a lot of financial planning material. Generally speaking, books either get too detailed and leave me overwhelmed—or too simple and leave me unsatisfied. Weaving Lucy's story into the book made theoretical concepts easily accessible and concrete. I felt that as a business owner myself, I could take actions to improve my business immediately."

Carl Brodie, Obisidian Advisory Group Inc.

"This informative book is a must read for the business owner. Save tax, manage risk, and enhance your estate through the alignment of ownership, business, and family. Marilyn deRooy-Pearson brings her wealth of knowledge and technical expertise to help you gain a detailed understanding of the importance of an integrated approach to financial, tax, and estate planning. In her words, STOP THE TAX LEAKAGE.*"*

Gordon P. Johnson, BA, CFP, President, Caris Financial Corp., Author of the Amazon #1 bestseller *Turn Your Mortgage Into a Pension*

Acknowledgements

If it were not for Krystine McInnis my book would not have been written and I would not have met the infallible Julie Salisbury. Thank you, Krystine.

To Julie, your vision is empowering and your dedication to be the best that you can be is invaluable.

To Ron Voyer and Richard Crosson, thank you for believing in me, for your support when I needed it most. My life, Vanessa's, and Zach's changed for the better because of you. Thank you.

To John Pearson, my husband, thank you for your support through my journey of writing this book. It means more than you know.

To my Mom, because of you, I have learned that I can climb every mountain. Thank you.

To the team at Influence Publishing, thank you for your patience, and support in getting my book to print!

Contents

Dedication

Testimonials

Acknowledgements

Preface

Chapter One: Introduction to the Parke Family............................ 1

Chapter Two: A New Business Partner 9

Chapter Three: Estate Freeze.. 15

Chapter Four: A New Business Structure.................................... 27

Chapter Five: Unanimous Shareholders Agreement 41

Chapter Six: Buy-Sell Funding... 59

Chapter Seven: Employee Retention.. 83

Chapter Eight: Wealth and Retirement Planning 89

Chapter Nine: Estate Planning... 103

Chapter Ten: Risk Management.. 115

Chapter Eleven: Putting It All Together 125

Chapter Twelve: Joint Ownership 139

Chapter Thirteen: Professional Corporations 147

Chapter Fourteen: The Business of Farming............................ 161

Workbook:.. 181

Author Biography:... 237

Further Information About the Author:................................... 239

Preface

Many business owners live with an uneasy feeling that there is something wrong with their financial wellbeing, but they just can't put their finger on it. They have accountants, lawyers, and investment and insurance advisors, so what are they missing?

Everything. Typically, each advisor, whether it is the accountant, lawyer, or other, works in isolation of the others, in independent silos. Although the business owner has trusted advisors who provide solid advice in their areas of expertise, there is little if no collaboration of planning among advisors. That causes uneasiness for the business owner.

This book is about alignment of ownership, business, and family. It is about minimizing tax leakage through effective corporate structures. It is about maximizing the hard-earned money of business owners to enjoy during their lifetimes. It is about leaving a legacy.

Family businesses make up a large portion of the Canadian economic and social landscape and the federal Government of Canada has recognized their positive impact on our economy. They have developed several tax incentives for family businesses. For example, the enhanced capital gains exemption for qualifying small businesses was to stimulate the creation of new businesses and the expansion of existing ones. The exemption originated at $20,000 in 1985, grew to $50,000 in 1986, and increased to $500,000 in 1988 as a result of the Federal Government's 1987 tax reform initiative. The enhanced capital gains exemption has since increased to $800,000 for 2014 and is indexed thereafter for inflation.

The Federal Government's initial objectives for the enhanced lifetime capital gains exemption included a desire to:

- promote economic growth and job creation by facilitating productive investment,
- increase participation by individuals in equity markets by providing incentives for risk taking and entrepreneurship,
- provide increased financing for Canadian corporations and, in particular, small businesses, and
- provide retirement income security for farmers and small business owners.

It appears that the Department of Finance has met its goal when you look at the current statistics according to Jennifer Halyk: "Approximately half of the Canadian workforce is employed by a family enterprise, and Canadian family enterprises create between 45 to 60 percent of [Canada's] Gross Domestic Product (GDP)." (*Research Matters in the Family Enterprise Field: Where Theory and Practise Meet*, Sauder School of Business, UBC Business Family Centre, October 3, 2012.)

A lot of what this book is about is not sexy or exciting, but it does bring government-sanctioned opportunities, rules, and regulations to the forefront. The business owner will be informed; learn how to increase tax efficiencies; get clarity and peace of mind.

In Chapters One through Eleven, I will explain the fundamentals of positioning your business to maximize the tax benefits available to qualified small business corporations using the example of the Parke Family and their business

WestCoast Outdoors Inc. While it is a fictitious company, it illustrates the fundamental options available to reduce the overall amount of tax business owners are paying.

In Chapters Twelve to Fourteen, I offer additional information on joint-ownership, family farms or fishing operations, and professional corporations. In addition, I offer you a workbook that you can use to explore and discover the tax savings available to you.

Lester R. Bittel said, "Good plans shape good decisions. That is why good planning helps to make elusive dreams come true" (*The Nine Master Keys of Management*).

Chapter One

Introduction to the Parke Family

"You can never get lost if you know where you are going."
Unknown

Meet the Parkes. Lucy Parke is married to Stan, her husband of twenty-five years. Ten years ago, Lucy founded WestCoast Outdoors Inc. (WestCoast). Lucy and her family's love for the outdoors was the catalyst for starting an outdoor clothing manufacturing company. Lucy is proud that WestCoast is a true Canadian company: all products are designed and manufactured in Canada. Lucy, with Stan's assistance in the start-up years, worked hard to get the business off the ground, slowly building it up to the national success it is today with sales of over $2 million.

Lucy and Stan have two teenage boys, Matt who is fifteen years old and Joe who is twelve. At this point, both Matt and Joe are focussed on sports activities and school. Both plan to attend post-secondary education. They both work at the manufacturing plant after school to earn spending money.

For the first two years, Stan assisted Lucy in establishing WestCoast; he then returned to his passion for computers and currently works for an international software company.

WestCoast is at a critical point. Lucy would like to grow WestCoast to sales of over $5 million, but to do so she requires additional capital for marketing and for expanding the manufacturing facility. Lucy's main concern is that she does not want to get into a large amount of debt for the expansion, but bringing in a new shareholder may be more difficult in the long run.

Stan is not prepared to give up his job to return to WestCoast, and neither of the boys are of an age to start thinking about taking over the business although Lucy would like to ensure that is a possibility down the road. When discussing her options, Lucy had some questions for me.

- What if I sell my business?
- What is it worth?
- What are the tax costs to selling my business?
- How can I pay less tax? I've worked hard for WestCoast's success.
- What if either Matt or Joe want to take over the business?
- Is it fair to sell it now, when it has been such a big part of our family?
- What are the implications of taking on a new business partner?
- Does he/she become a shareholder?

Getting Lucy's business house in order is paramount to her future career. We delve into the implications of adding a business partner, because true to her heart she would love to take WestCoast to the next level.

As Lucy prepares for the sale of a portion of her business, both Lucy and Stan explore the answers to two fundamental questions:

1. What is the Parkes' current financial situation?
2. Where do Lucy and Stan want to be in ten or fifteen years?

The planning process involves building a bridge between where they are today and where they want to be in the future. This involves a "living" approach to the planning process—undertaken while Lucy and Stan are alive, healthy, and in control. It requires an examination of and planning for two possible scenarios:

1. Events proceed as Lucy and Stan hope and anticipate they will.
2. An unanticipated event occurs—this includes premature death, incapacity, insolvency, and matrimonial breakdown.

This process is not static. People's lives and circumstances change. Tax, probate, and other laws change on a regular basis. It is important that the Parkes' plan be monitored and updated as necessary and on a periodic basis.

After our initial meeting, Lucy and Stan spent considerable time discussing and determining what their objectives were. At our next meeting, they provided us with these objectives:

- to plan for the possibility of the addition of a new equity shareholder ensuring that WestCoast's growth and value to date attributes to Lucy. Any change in structure should also be a good foundation for Lucy and Stan's retirement and succession.
- to provide an effective strategy through which to transfer ownership of WestCoast
- to securitize and protect the financial position of the Parkes family on a go-forward basis to ensure their lifestyles are guaranteed
- to assist with their sons' post-secondary educations in a tax-effective manner
- to plan for unanticipated events including claims by creditors, incapacity, possible future matrimonial breakdown, and premature death
- to minimize taxes, professional fees, and other costs associated with the ongoing management and ultimate disposition of their estate

In reviewing the Parkes' planning options, we note that Lucy, Stan, and their children are Canadian residents for tax purposes. More specifically, we note that no individuals are citizens of the United States of America (US).

There are many differences between US and Canadian tax laws. Some of the most important distinctions from a Canadian's perspective are as follows:

- Canadian citizens are taxed based on their residency status. If they have emigrated from Canada, Canadian citizens are subject to Canadian tax only on income earned in Canada. US citizens, green card holders, and "deemed residents for tax purposes" are taxed on their worldwide income regardless of where they reside. If a US citizen lives outside the US, they are still required to file an annual US tax return that includes their income earned worldwide.
- Canada does not have an estate tax.
- The US does have an estate tax.

Although the process of determining your residency status in the US is arduous and complicated, Chapter 15 – Workbook has a worksheet that will provide some guidance as to whether or not you should seek professional advice from a US tax expert. If in doubt, please seek professional advice.

The Parke Family Genome

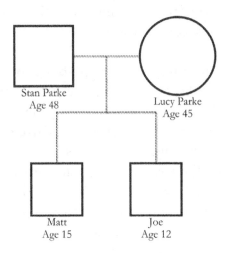

Stan Parke
Age 48

Lucy Parke
Age 45

Matt
Age 15

Joe
Age 12

WestCoast's Current Corporate Structure

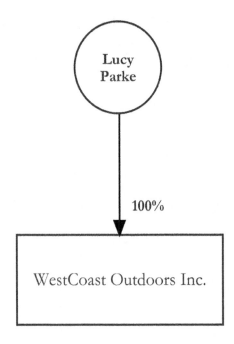

Lucy
Parke

100%

WestCoast Outdoors Inc.

In this chapter, we have discussed

- the importance of creating goals and objectives
- the effect of citizenship, specifically US citizenship, when planning
- assessing where you are today and where you want to be tomorrow

In Chapter Fifteen – Workbook, you will find additional information

- personal information gathering
- recording your family genome
- United States residency status – Is there need for concern?

Chapter Two

A New Business Partner

Lucy plans substantial growth for WestCoast; she believes that a new business partner who complements her strengths would be the best way to move WestCoast forward.

Although Lucy has made this decision, she does have some important concerns:

- She does not want to give up control of WestCoast.
- She wants to realize the equity she has built up in her company.
- If she were to sell a percentage of her WestCoast shares, she wonders how much would she likely get for it.
- She wonders what are the steps to get WestCoast ready for a partial sale of her business.

When considering the addition of a new partner, it is important that Lucy have her business in order, so that it is properly positioned for a potential new business partner. This involves the co-operation of her operations manager and key employee, Zoey. Given the confidentiality of this process, it is imperative that Lucy have an employment agreement drafted that protects Zoey's employment and her confidentiality throughout the process. As Lucy expected, Zoey was open and helpful in preparing WestCoast for the addition of a new business partner.

Lucy has some anxiety, of course; WestCoast has been a big part of her life for many years. Finding the right business partner is crucial to the next phase of WestCoast's growth. It is important, therefore, to go through the process of ensuring that WestCoast and, more importantly, she herself is prepared for the addition of a new partner and the growth of the business.

It takes a great deal of effort to prepare a business for sale or partial sale. At the very least, Lucy will be spending time analyzing her business and enhancing its value. A strong management team translates to a well-organized business. Not only is this beneficial for attracting a new shareholder, but it is a strong foundation for the growth Lucy has planned for WestCoast.

A critical look at the business is important. What areas are strong and what areas need improvement? This process is not to criticize past performance, but to look at opportunities for the future. Addressing areas that improve the marketability of your business is important. Areas to focus on for improvement are:

Sales and profitability—What are your profit margins? When was the last time prices were increased? Is there an opportunity to do so now? How efficient is the production of the product? Is there an opportunity to cut costs without cutting quality?

Strong management structure—Ideally, knowledge and talent are not concentrated in only a few individuals. Does the management organization make sense? Is management positioned for growth? How are business decisions made? Have operational systems been documented?

Diversity in customers and suppliers—Strong concentration of either can affect the value of the business.

Removal of all non-operating assets such as cash and investments—These can be transferred to another company on a tax-deferred basis. This will also assist in the qualification of the $800,000 capital gains exemption (2014) available to shareholders of qualifying shares.

Potential transfer of land and buildings to a separate company—This is mainly for creditor protection, but also to decrease the purchase price of the shares.

Technology—Are your systems up to date? Do you have a proper recovery program to minimize losses in case of disruption? Are your systems generating productive management information or do you wish you had more information at your disposal to make effective decisions?

Tax issues—Are the corporate tax filings up to date, including income tax, payroll remittances, GST, and PST? Are you maximizing all tax credits available to you? Consider Research and Development tax credits for example.

It is important to have the business ready for sale, but just as important is your preparation as a shareholder to mitigate taxes at time of sale. We spoke with Lucy about the tax implications of the various ways to transact her sale. We looked at her current structure as well as potential changes to effect the sale. These are our objectives:

- minimize tax leakage on the sale
- realize the equity in WestCoast that Lucy has built to date
- protect the Parke family assets
- maximize the Parke family's wealth

The following two options were presented to Lucy for her consideration:

1. Restructure WestCoast's current shareholdings. This would allow for West Coast's future growth to go to Lucy's family, not simply to her as a shareholder.
2. Sell a percentage of Lucy's shares and continue with the current structure.

The second option, although more cost-effective, will not address most of Lucy and Stan's objectives for today and most certainly not for the future. As a result, together we determined to focus on restructuring WestCoast to ensure that Lucy and Stan's goals and objectives are met. In addition, this will allow Lucy the flexibility to decide when she would like to introduce a new shareholder.

In this chapter, we have discussed

Getting reading for the partial sale of your business from an operational perspective includes consideration of the following:

- a strong management structure
- diversity in customers and suppliers
- technology
- tax issues

In Chapter Fifteen – Workbook, you will find additional information

- getting your business ready for sale
- what are your financial statements are telling you?

Chapter Three

Estate Freeze

As Lucy is preparing the day-to-day operations of WestCoast for a new shareholder and future growth, it is equally important that Lucy's overall corporate structure meet her needs to mitigate taxes at sale and allow for the long-term family and estate planning needs.

Through our review of Lucy's current concerns and objectives and the Parke family's needs, a corporate restructuring will provide the foundation from which we can plan to meet the Parke family's current and long-term objectives. These objectives are to:

- minimize tax leakage on sale,
- realize the equity in WestCoast that Lucy has built to date,
- provide for post-secondary education costs for both Matt and Joe,
- protect the Parke family assets, and
- maximize the Parke family's wealth.

For Lucy, a significant portion of her and her family's net worth is in the value of her WestCoast shares. An estate freeze is perhaps the single most important estate planning structure for incorporated businesses and, coupled with creating a family trust, this is an effective strategy to secure WestCoast's assets and plan for the family's future. In addition, with WestCoast's anticipated appreciation in value, the estate freeze allows Lucy to start transferring the future increase in WestCoast's value to all her family members today.

Implementing the freeze now will not impede Lucy's ability to earn substantial income going forward. It provides an orderly transition of wealth, generates significant short- and long-term tax savings, and assists in securing and protecting the financial position of the Parke family.

An estate freeze means locking in WestCoast's existing value in the common shares held by Lucy. This allows Lucy to retain the equity she has built up over the past ten years. The related tax liability will be payable when Lucy dies or when she otherwise disposes of the freeze-preferred shares she receives as a result of the freeze. If Lucy's will stipulates that the WestCoast shares pass to Stan, then the tax liability occurs when Stan passes away.

Through the freeze, new WestCoast "growth" shares are issued to the Parke Family Trust, for the benefit of Lucy, Stan, their two sons, and any future grandchildren. The estate freeze occurs without any immediate tax consequences to Lucy or other family members.

There are many advantages to an estate freeze. An estate freeze:

- is the first step in establishing a succession plan for the benefit of Lucy and her family.
- allows for flexibility in estate planning for Lucy and Stan and their children using a discretionary family trust.
- allows Lucy to retain the value of WestCoast that she has built to date.
- purifies WestCoast's "small business corporation" status.
- facilitates small business expansion planning.
- allows Lucy to remain in control of all corporate assets for as long as she wishes.
- allows for income splitting with family members.
- mitigates any capital gains tax on the last to die of Stan and Lucy.
- multiplies the availability of the enhanced capital gains exemption.
- crystallizes capital gains for the enhanced capital gains exemption.
- allows for an orderly, systematic redemption of shares following retirement.
- reduces creditor risk by removing the "growth" value from potential attachment by creditors of Lucy, Stan, and their children.

To the extent that capital assets are owned at the operating company level, they are completely exposed to liability and other claims by general business creditors. WestCoast carries on normal business activity, and a large portion of the value of WestCoast is represented by capital assets based on their latest financial statements. These assets, land, the warehouse building, and cash and investments are completely exposed to potential claims by creditors and, in the current legal environment, this represents liability exposure.

Therefore, Lucy will transfer the excess cash and investments she has accumulated in WestCoast, on a tax-deferred basis, to a newly created holding company, HoldCo. She is implementing this transfer for creditor protection as well as wanting to keep the assets for her family.

In addition, Lucy likes the flexibility of maintaining ownership of the land and the building WestCoast occupies, rather than including them in the sale of WestCoast shares. As a result, she will transfer them to a newly created company, BuildCo. Over time, she will be able to assess whether or not she will sell a percentage of BuildCo shares to her new business partner. For the time being, she is happy that her family will enjoy any growth in value through ownership of the family trust.

The advantages of the land and building transfer are several:

- ensures Lucy maintains 100 percent ownership of land and buildings
- increases flexibility
- provides protection from creditors (unless transferred in anticipation of a lawsuit or other legal claim)
- decreases WestCoast's share price
- ensures that, even after retirement, Lucy can receive rental income on the property, providing her with another source of retirement income

The two drawbacks of the transfer are:

- the new shareholder may also want to own the land and building as part of the buy in
- because WestCoast's share price is lower, Lucy may be looking for more funds to facilitate WestCoast's growth

The estate freeze will not only include the creation of a new holding company, a new building company, and a family trust, but also the transfer of excess cash and investments into HoldCo, and the transfer of the land and the building into BuildCo.

The preferred shares Lucy receives for the equity she has built up in WestCoast to date will have a redemption value equal to the Fair Market Value of WestCoast. The freeze also allows the newly created family trust, HoldCo, and BuildCo to subscribe for WestCoast shares at a nominal value. Lucy will maintain control of WestCoast as trustee of the family trust. In conjunction with the freeze, Lucy will crystallize her unused capital gains exemption allowing her access to a maximum of $800,000 of tax-free capital gains on her WestCoast shares.

Business Valuations

Having WestCoast valued is an essential part of Lucy and Stan's estate and wealth management planning. In addition, tax legislation requires that the various transactions involved in an estate freeze, such as Lucy is about to undertake, all occur at fair market value.

Under common law terms, fair market value is defined as the highest price in terms of cash that would be paid by an informed and prudent investor, acting at arm's length, under no compulsion to transact, in an open and unrestricted market. Basically, fair market value is a reasonable price that an unrelated person would pay for your business.

The Canada Revenue Agency (CRA) increasingly relies on Chartered Business Valuators (CBVs) in assessing valuation issues. The CBVs employed by the CRA are bound by the same standards and guidelines as all CBVs. Having your business valued by a CBV will reduce your risk of a reassessment; the valuation will be prepared using standards and valuation techniques familiar to CRA valuators.

An independent business valuation is an essential part of the estate freeze process, because it:

- documents the intention of the parties to transact at fair market value,
- ensures the basis for the market value is fair and reasonable, and
- ensures CRA will understand the valuation approach taken in the circumstances.

An important part of the restructuring is the creation of a new holding company—HoldCo. This holding company has the following advantages, because it allows for:

- creditor protection of WestCoast's retained earnings,
- varying shareholder compensation needs,
- wealth accumulation, and
- preservation of the capital gains exemption.

Creditor Protection

Through the use of tax-free intercorporate dividends, excess cash and retained earnings can be moved to HoldCo. Generally speaking, when the holding company owns more than 10 percent of the shares of WestCoast, dividends are received tax-free by the holding company.

The assets held in HoldCo are protected from WestCoast's creditors, unless the shareholders have provided guarantees on behalf of WestCoast. This is based on current law.

Varying Shareholder Compensation and Wealth Accumulation

Individuals have different income needs based on their personal circumstances. When profits are distributed to the shareholders via dividends, income is received by each shareholder. If no holding company exists to facilitate tax deferral, the shareholder is required to pay taxes on the income received at his/her tax rate. Lucy, however, has the option to either take the income personally and pay tax, or defer taking the income personally and investing it in her holding company. Essentially, Lucy is now using after-tax small-business dollars to start investing for the future rather than using after-tax personal dollars to invest.

Currently, the small business tax rate in Canada (for the first $500,000 of taxable income, ranges from 13 percent to 15.5 percent. There are exceptions, Manitoba's rate is for the first $425,000 and Nova Scotia's rate is for the first $350,000. Quebec's tax rate is 19 percent). Top marginal tax rates for individuals in Canada range from 39 percent to 50 percent (Quebec's rate is 54.75%). For example, a business owner in the top marginal tax bracket in Saskatchewan is taxed at 44 percent, yet his corporation is taxed at 13 percent, yielding a 31 percent deferred tax savings that can be invested within the holding company. Saskatchewan's tax rates are used throughout this book, because the rates are reflective of an average rate for Canada's provinces. Based on a salary of $100,000, a business owner will have $31,000 more to invest if the funds are invested in a holding company such as HoldCo, maximizing their tax deferral.

Investing the retained earnings of a corporation makes excellent sense, because in addition to having more to invest, generally speaking, passive investment income (rent, interest, royalties), capital gains, and portfolio dividends are taxed at virtually the same tax rate regardless of whether the income is earned by a corporation and distributed to a shareholder or earned by the individual directly. This is the theory of tax integration. However, because every province has its own tax rate, integration is not a perfect science. When taking into account the ability to use after-tax corporate dollars for investing, tax deferral mechanisms, and the use of a holding company to invest, the shareholder will have more investment dollars and, therefore, a larger investment portfolio, all things being equal.

The following diagram illustrates the tax advantage of reinvesting $100 dollars in HoldCo rather than paying personal tax and investing the after-tax balance. In this example, Lucy has $100 that she has earmarked for investing. If Lucy chooses to take $100 out of the company and invest the net after-tax amount she receives, she will have $56 to invest. Alternatively, if Lucy transfers the $100 of after-tax corporate dollars to HoldCo, she has $87 to invest. The net increase in investment dollars is $31.

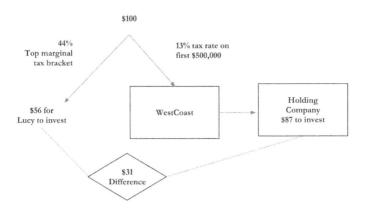

$100

44%
Top marginal
tax bracket

13% tax rate on
first $500,000

$56 for
Lucy to invest

WestCoast

Holding
Company
$87 to invest

$31
Difference

Saskatchewan 2014 tax rates

Capital Gains Exemption

In addition, the holding company facilitates WestCoast's ability to maintain its "qualified small business corporation" status (QSBC). Tax-free intercorporate dividends from WestCoast to HoldCo allow WestCoast to transfer excess cash to HoldCo on a tax-free basis. The funds can be invested. In addition, if WestCoast requires the funds in the future, HoldCo, through a tax-free intercorporate dividend, can transfer the funds back to WestCoast.

Being a QSBC is important because it qualifies its shareholders for the $800,000 (2014) enhanced capital gains exemption on the sale of its shares. Essentially, the first $800,000 gain on the sale of QSBC shares is sheltered from tax. It is important to note that the $800,000 is a personal lifetime exemption, so if any or all of the exemption has been used by an individual on a previous QSBC share sale, only the remainder, up to $800,000 (2014 maximum personal exemption amount) can be applied to the current share sale.

To qualify as a QSBC, the company must meet the following four criteria:

1. Throughout a period of twenty-four months immediately preceding the trigger date, the shares must not have been owned by any person or partnership other than an individual who is related to him or her. There is an exemption to this requirement. Shareholders of newly incorporated small business corporations have access to the special exemption of QSBC shares even when the corporation has existed for less than twenty-four months. Related to this exemption, a sole proprietor can utilize the capital gains exemption available to qualified shares of a small business corporation by rolling the assets into a newly formed corporation under Section 85 of the *Income Tax Act* (Canada) and subsequently sell the shares.

2. The company must be a Canadian Controlled Private Corporation (CCPC). That is, 50 percent or more of the shares must be owned by Canadian residents for tax purposes. Also, the shares must not be traded on the stock exchange.

3. Ninety percent or more of the Fair Market Value of the assets of the company must be used in active business at trigger date. Any investments that are not directly required for the day-to-day running

of the business are considered passive assets. If the Fair Market Value of these assets is greater than 10 percent, the CCPC will not qualify as a QSBC. A trigger date is the sale of the business, death of the shareholder, or restructuring of the company.

4. Fifty percent or more of the Fair Market Value of the assets of the company must be used in active business immediately preceding twenty-four months prior to the trigger date.

In this chapter, we have discussed

- the benefits of an estate freeze
- importance of a proper business valuation
- Qualified Small Business Share criteria
- the benefits of creating a holding company

In this chapter, we have discussed the tax savings

For the shareholder:

- tax deferral related to investing within the corporation structure by transferring after-tax corporate dollars via tax-free intercorporate dividends to a holding company for investing, a savings of approximately 30 percent depending on your province of residence
- ensuring that the operating company maintain its qualified small business corporation status so that its shares qualify for the $800,000 tax-free capital gains treatment

In Chapter Fifteen–Workbook, you will find additional information

- the main advantages of an estate freeze
- qualified small business corporation status

Chapter Four

A New Business Structure

WestCoast's Current Corporate Structure

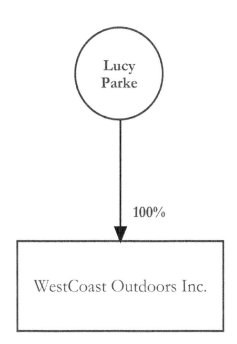

Based on the discussions we have had with Lucy and Stan, we have determined that Lucy is going to proceed with a restructuring of WestCoast Outdoors Inc. WestCoast's new structure will include:

- the creation of a new holding company for wealth and estate planning purposes.
- a new building company that will own the corporate land and buildings.
- a discretionary family trust that will facilitate income splitting and estate planning.

The objectives of the WestCoast restructuring include:

- flexibility of estate planning for Lucy, Stan, and their children using a discretionary family trust,
- creditor proofing of WestCoast's business,
- accommodation for future shareholder buy-in,
- purification of WestCoast's "small business corporation" status,
- preservation and multiplication of the Parke family capital gains deductions on any future sale of WestCoast, and
- mitigation of any capital gains tax on the last to die of Lucy and Stan.

The Proposed Structure for WestCoast

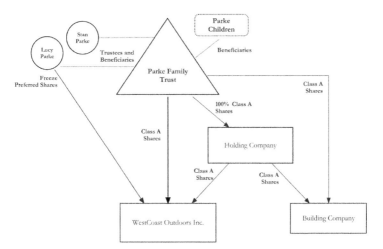

In order to meet Lucy and Stan's objectives listed above, an estate freeze will be implemented. There are various ways of accomplishing an estate freeze and the following is not a complete list of steps but provides an overview of how a freeze is accomplished.

Step One: Creation of the Parke Family Trust

The first step is the creation of a trust for the Parke family as the vehicle to accumulate future wealth for the benefit of Lucy and her family. In addition, when the children reach the age of majority, they can receive tax-efficient income distributions. A trust is a legal relationship between three parties: the settlor, the trustees, and the beneficiaries. In order to "settle" a trust (to create a trust), an individual (the settlor) has an asset to be held in trust for specified individuals (the beneficiaries). The trustees are responsible for the management of the assets held within the trust, and distribution of either capital or income to the beneficiaries. The rules to create a trust date back to old British trust rules that still exist today.

The creation of the Parke Family Trust includes the following three steps:

1. The Parke Family Trust is to be settled by Lucy's mother, Victoria, with a silver coin. Victoria has the asset that she wishes to be held in trust for the benefit of the Parke Family. The silver coin or the funds with which to purchase the silver coin must come from the settlor, Victoria, and under no circumstances is Lucy to compensate her mother, the settlor of the trust, for creating the trust. The silver coin will be attached to the trust documents and remain there until the trust is wound up. This coin is what legally creates the trust.

2. Lucy and Stan are appointed as the original trustees of the Parke Family Trust. The trust documents have a provision that allows Lucy and Stan to remove and add trustees during their lifetime. The majority of the trustees must be Canadian residents at all times to ensure the trust meets the Canadian residency status requirements. The trust document gives the trustees complete discretion in the management of trust assets.

3. The trustees open a bank account on behalf of the trust. The trustees arrange for the trust to borrow funds from an arm's length person or entity on commercial terms without guarantees. These funds will be used to acquire shares of WestCoast and the newly incorporated companies HoldCo and BuildCo.

This step is important to ensure that the trust is not inadvertently put offside of the trust rules. This would result in the loss of the benefits we are trying to achieve by establishing the trust.

Step Two: Amendment of WestCoast's Share Capital

WestCoast's share capital will be amended to facilitate the issuance of various new classes of shares during the estate freeze.

Step Three: Share Exchange

Lucy will exchange her WestCoast common shares for new WestCoast Class C preferred shares. The new Class C shares represent 100 percent of the fair market value of WestCoast.

Step Four: Creation of a Holding Company

The creation of HoldCo is executed to facilitate:

* creditor protection of WestCoast's retained earnings,
* wealth accumulation,
* preservation of capital gains exemption, and
* allowance for varying shareholder compensation needs.

Step Five: Creation of a Building Company

The purpose of creating a separate building company is to:

- ensure Lucy maintains 100 percent ownership of land and buildings,
- increase flexibility,
- provide protection from creditors (unless transferred in anticipation of a lawsuit or other legal claim),
- decrease WestCoast's share price, and
- ensure that, even after retirement, Lucy can receive rental income on the property, providing her with another source of retirement income.

Step Six: Subscription for Shares

The Parke Family Trust subscribes for the following participating shares:

- WestCoast Class A voting shares
- HoldCo Class A voting shares
- BuildCo Class A voting shares

The funds used to purchase these shares come from the borrowed money as per Step One. This share ownership structure allows for the payment of dividends from WestCoast, HoldCo, and BuildCo to the family trust to be disbursed to the beneficiaries as declared by the trustees.

HoldCo subscribes to the following participating shares:

- WestCoast Class A voting shares
- BuildCo Class A voting shares

HoldCo's investment in WestCoast and BuildCo of over 10 percent of the shares allows for intercorporate tax-free dividends to be paid from each company to HoldCo.

Various other transactions occur to execute the estate freeze, none of which will be detailed here, because they are beyond the scope of this book.

The estate freeze is a well-recognized tool that has been used in tax and estate planning as well as in income splitting transactions for many years.

Lucy's estate freeze involves the exchange of her WestCoast common shares for non-participating fixed value shares (preferred shares) on a tax-deferred basis in accordance with one of the many rollover provisions of the *Income Tax Act* (Canada). Once the share exchange is complete, WestCoast's fair market value is attributable to these newly issued fixed-value preferred shares, allowing new participating shares to be issued from WestCoast's treasury for a nominal price to the Parke Family Trust and HoldCo.

The Parke Family Trust's ownership of the new WestCoast shares allows for the future growth of the company to accrue to any or all of the beneficiaries of the trust. In addition, future dividends can also be paid from WestCoast via the trust to any or all of the beneficiaries of the trust. This is a great way to fund Lucy's children's post-secondary education with after-tax business dollars and at the child's low tax rate.

Two of the more significant benefits of an estate freeze are the potential deferral of tax and the ability to income split. Tax deferral is achieved through investing after-tax corporate dollars, which are significantly lower than individual shareholders paying themselves and then investing the cash once all taxes have been paid.

Income splitting uses the same after-tax corporate

dollars as tax deferral does, but rather than keeping the funds within the corporate structure, the company pays dividends to adult trust beneficiaries who are at a substantially lower tax rate than the shareholder. If an adult trust beneficiary has no other source of income in a taxation year, they can receive approximately $25,000 of tax-free dividends (Manitoba and Prince Edward Island are exceptions, at approximately $15,000). The actual amount is dependent on your province of residence. In the Parke family's situation, this is a great way to fund post-secondary education for the boys.

The following chart illustrates the benefits of income splitting with a family member who is in a lower income tax bracket than the business owner. In Lucy's situation, income splitting with her son, Matt, once he is over seventeen years of age, provides an additional $31 of funds for every $100 withdrawn from the corporation. For every $100 Lucy withdraws from WestCoast and pays tax at her tax rate of 44 percent, she would have $56 available to fund Matt's post-secondary education. Alternatively, for every $100 withdrawn from WestCoast and paid to Matt as beneficiary of the Parke Family Trust, he will have $87 to fund his education. Income splitting through a family trust is a widely used vehicle for business owners to fund adult children's post-secondary education.

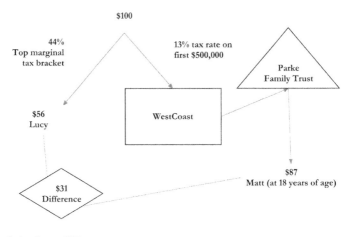

$100

44%
Top marginal
tax bracket

13% tax rate on
first $500,000

Parke
Family Trust

$56
Lucy

WestCoast

$87
Matt (at 18 years of age)

$31
Difference

Saskatchewan 2014 tax rates

The chart on the following page illustrates the benefits of tax deferral when building personal wealth using a holding company to invest in after-tax corporate dollars. Similar to the chart above illustrating the benefits of income splitting, this chart illustrates the benefits of tax deferral. For every $100 withdrawn from WestCoast and paid to Lucy, the funds available to Lucy for investing are $56. If Lucy were to transfer the funds to HoldCo for investing, Lucy would have $87 to invest. The result is 31 percent more dollars available for investing at the holding company level versus paying the money to the shareholder .

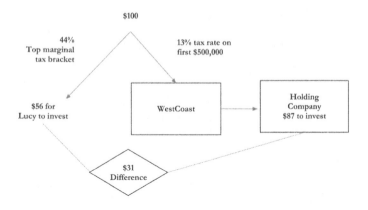

$100

44%
Top marginal
tax bracket

13% tax rate on
first $500,000

$56 for
Lucy to invest

WestCoast

Holding
Company
$87 to invest

$31
Difference

Saskatchewan 2014 tax rates

In addition to the tax savings available to Lucy during her lifetime, the estate freeze also provides tax relief at death. Provisions in the *Income Tax Act* (Canada) deem an individual to have disposed of all of their capital property held at the time immediately before their passing for proceeds equal to the fair market value of each property. The main exception to this rule is that any capital property transferred to a spouse or a qualifying spousal trust is deemed by the *Income Tax Act* (Canada) to take place at the original cost of the asset resulting in the deferral of any capital gain that would otherwise be realized until the second spouse passes.

In Lucy's case, her only assets related to WestCoast are the fixed-value preferred shares that she received at the time of the estate freeze. Depending on the time of her death, Lucy may have redeemed these preferred shares to supplement her retirement income, paying taxes as she redeems the shares. For every redemption, her date-of-death tax liability is reduced so the tax consequences at death may be minimal. If Lucy predeceases Stan the tax liability will pass on to Stan.

Lucy's tax liability has been fixed with regards to her business asset, WestCoast shares. A cost-effective way to plan for date-of-death taxes is to use other people's money—that is, life insurance. Typically, life insurance costs pennies on the dollar for coverage and Lucy's estate will not be faced with the possibility of having to liquidate other estate assets to pay the taxes owing on her preferred shares.

The benefits of Lucy's new business structure are quite attractive; however, it is imperative that the execution of the estate freeze is carried out by qualified tax and legal professionals to ensure compliance with all the rules of the *Income Tax Act* (Canada).

In this chapter, we have discussed

- the proposed new business structure for Lucy
- general steps of an estate freeze:
  - * Step One: Creation of the Parke Family Trust
  - * Step Two: Amendment of WestCoast's Share Capital
  - * Step Three: Share Exchange
  - * Step Four: Creation of a Holding Company
  - * Step Five: Creation of a Building Company
  - * Step Six: Subscription for Shares

In this chapter, we have discussed the tax savings

For the shareholder:

- Tax deferral when building personal wealth using a holding company to invest in after-tax corporate dollars. The result is approximately 30 percent more dollars available (depending on your province of residence) for investing at the holding company level versus paying the money to the shareholder who in turn pays personal tax and then invests the balance.
- The family trust provides a vehicle with which income splitting can occur without ownership of the corporation's shares. Through income splitting with a family member (over the age of seventeen) who is in a lower income tax bracket than the business owner, there is approximately a $30 cash flow increase for every $100 paid (depending on your province of residence).
- The shareholder's exchange of growth shares for

freeze fixed value preferred shares defines the actual taxes payable upon death if all shares are still owned by the shareholder. The future growth of the company is attributed to the family trust shares.

In Chapter Fifteen – Workbook, you will find additional information

- discretionary family trusts

Chapter Five

Unanimous Shareholders Agreement

Once Lucy has sold her shares and she has a new shareholder, she and her new business partner, as the shareholders of the company, should draft a Unanimous Shareholders Agreement (USA). In addition, both their wills should be updated to include the new corporate structure and assets. It is important that the wills, the USA, and the corporate structure are congruent.

In addition to the various topics to be covered in a USA, as a result of an existing freeze, the shareholders should also include a clause in the agreement that allows the owners to require the corporation to undertake a refreeze at the owners' request. Such an agreement avoids the requirement of having to obtain shareholder consent to a reorganization at a time in the future when the shareholders may not all be in agreement on a particular course of action.

A USA is the Will of a company. It sets out the wishes of the shareholders. Many shareholders start a business and get into the running and growing of the business believing that a common goal and relationship will get them through any issues that may arise down the road. As we all know, that is typically not how things work out. Preparing a USA at the start of the business or business relationship—when

41

relationships are good and business growth is exciting and the common unity of the shareholders—is the best time to set out the process for when things don't go according to plan.

There are numerous objectives for a USA, but most importantly, it creates liquidity for mostly illiquid shares of a private company. Failure to provide a smooth transition could result in financial hardship for the departing shareholder or his/her estate, and could result in uneasiness among employees, suppliers, and creditors of the business. A properly funded USA reassures the creditors of the financial health of the business and of the remaining shareholders.

The USA outlines how the business will continue under each of the following six conditions:

- upon the death of a shareholder
- upon disability of a shareholder
- upon a critical illness of a shareholder
- upon disagreement between shareholders
- upon divorce of a shareholder
- upon retirement of a shareholder

It also provides a market for the seller and, if properly funded, the funds for the buyer. It provides security for the deceased's family and heirs, allowing the heirs to receive the Fair Market Value for their share of the business. And it also provides the ability for the surviving shareholders to continue operating the business. When a USA is properly funded, the remaining shareholders receive the funds, which can be used to continue with the business, maintaining the stability of the business.

USAs are usually drawn up by corporate lawyers. When a shareholder dispute arises however, a litigator takes over and they either try to resolve the dispute or they take the issue to court. Consider a different approach to USAs. Determine what the objective of the agreement is, and start the document with that objective. This gives the opposing parties a basis with which to start the discussions; it gives the courts guidance as to the overall objective of the agreement. Remember, the USA is signed by all shareholders, so they are all aware of the purpose and objectives of the agreement.

Regardless of the triggering event, the following criteria should be considered:

- a specific definition of the triggering event. Death as a triggering event leaves nothing to interpretation. However, disability, critical illness, and disputes between shareholders can have a different definition for each shareholder. More guidance given to these definitions in the USA results in a clearer interpretation at a trigger date.
- a clearly defined valuation method. Should a dispute arise, an arbitration method should be described.
- a clearly defined method of how the share purchase will be financed. If insurance products are to be used, the ownership of the insurance and the requirement to maintain a policy should be written into the agreement.
- an integrated approach to the tax planning that allows for changes in tax rules, for example: an increase in the capital gains exemption amount, stop-loss rules, and eligible dividends.

Definitions of Six Triggering Events

Death

A fundamental decision shareholders need to make is who must buy the company shares when a death occurs. It is important to understand the difference between a circumstance where the company redeems shares or buys the shares for cancellation from the estate ("share redemption") and a circumstance in which the remaining shareholders buy them ("share purchase"). Typically, the choice is driven by income tax consequences.

A **share redemption** results in a deemed dividend to the deceased's estate. If there are life insurance proceeds and the USA requires the use of the capital dividend account, the life insurance proceeds are paid tax-free to the estate via the capital dividend account. They may be subject to stop-loss rules. A capital gain is not triggered in a share redemption and there is no ability for the deceased to utilize the $800,000 tax-free capital gains exemption on the shares.

A **share purchase** from the estate by the surviving shareholders will result in a potential capital gain to the deceased's date-of-death tax return. If the shares are Qualified Small Business Corporation shares and the deceased has not utilized all of his/her capital gains exemption, then the deceased has up to $800,000 (2014) in tax-free capital gain exemptions available to offset against any capital gain triggered at death.

Utilization of the enhanced capital gains exemption provides $800,000 of tax-free capital gains to the owner of qualified business corporation shares (QSBC).

It is important to note that access to the capital gains exemption may be limited or denied if the shareholder has either cumulative net investment losses or an allowable business investment loss. Both of these losses erode the benefits of the capital gains exemption.

Cumulative net investment losses (CNIL) are the balance of cumulative investment expenses claimed in excess of investment income (since 1987). Investment expenses include interest expenses and carrying charges. Investment income might include taxable dividends, rent, and royalties.

The taxable capital gains that otherwise qualify for the capital gains exemption will be reduced by the CNIL balance; that is the excess of the cumulative investment expenses less the cumulative investment income.

A common strategy to mitigate the impact of a CNIL balance is to declare dividends from the shareholder's private corporation when his/her cumulative investment expenses are becoming increasingly large, eliminating the CNIL balance.

Ideally, the USA has enough flexibility to provide for the specific tax-planning opportunities of the deceased shareholder. Ideally, the estate dictates the tax results. That is, is there a share purchase or a share redemption or a combination of the two methods maximizing the tax planning opportunities?

Considerations When Using Life Insurance as a USA Funding Source

If life insurance is the funding method for the buy-sell agreement, consider including provisions in the USA that mandate the use of the corporation's capital dividend account. In the Ontario case *Ribeiro Estate v. Braun Nursery Limited et al* (Court file number: 06-25122), the surviving shareholders successfully argued that, although the USA required the use of insurance proceeds to buy the deceased's estate's shares, the estate had no entitlement to the capital dividend account. The share redemption, therefore, was a taxable dividend. Silence on the use of the capital dividend account had unfavourable tax consequences to Ribeiro's estate.

When drafting the USA, shareholders should consider two separate issues regarding use of insurance proceeds upon the death of a shareholder:

- Who is entitled to the insurance proceeds?
- Who is entitled to the tax benefit of the capital dividend account?

Typically, the answer to the first question is the estate of the deceased; however, there may be compelling arguments for both the estate and the surviving shareholders regarding the benefit of the capital dividend account.

The Ribeiro case stresses that it is critical not to be silent in the shareholders' agreement about the entitlement to the company's capital dividend account that results from its increase due to the receipt of insurance proceeds from a shareholder's death.

Considerations Regarding Eligible and Non-Eligible Dividends

Effective 2006, Canada's dividend regime changed. Taxable dividends in Canada are designated as either eligible dividends or non-eligible dividends. Eligible dividends are dividends received by a person who is a resident of Canada, paid after 2005 by a corporation resident in Canada and designated to be an eligible dividend.

For CCPCs, to qualify as an eligible dividend, the dividend must be paid out of the corporation's General Rate Income Pool (GRIP). GRIP is a pool that accumulates when a CCPC pays the general rate of income tax on active business income. More specifically, CCPCs that generate active business income are eligible for the small business tax rate (in 2014, the tax rate ranged from 13 percent to 15.5 percent, and was at 19 percent in Quebec) for the first $500,000 of taxable income. In Manitoba, the small business tax rate is applicable to taxable income up to $425,000 and in Nova Scotia, taxable income up to $350,000 (2104 tax rates). Any taxable income above $500,000 (or $425, 000 in Manitoba and $350,000 in Nova Scotia) is taxed at the general rate; in 2014, the general tax rate ranged from 25 percent to 31 percent. Income subject to the general rate of tax is added to GRIP. The calculation of GRIP is beyond the scope of this book; however, it is important to know that because of the concept of integration, the higher general tax rate for CCPCs results in potential "eligible dividends," which are taxed to the shareholder at a lower rate. In Saskatchewan the difference in the shareholder's personal tax rate is 10.1 percent—24.81 percent for eligible dividends versus 34.91 percent for non-eligible dividends (2014 tax rates).

In a USA, it is therefore also important to address whether or not a deemed dividend that arises as a result of a share redemption is being paid in whole or in part out of the company's GRIP as an eligible dividend. If it is "in part," then the extent of the payment should also be defined. Silence on GRIP can lead to conflict and potential lawsuits between the surviving shareholders and the trustees of the deceased's estate.

Surviving Spouse

In 1995, the federal government implemented Stop Loss Rules, effectively allowing only 50 percent of any losses incurred by a deceased shareholder's estate to be carried back to his/her terminal return. Because of the Stop Loss Rules (see Chapter 15 for a more detailed explanation), it is important that a USA be more flexible to ensure maximum tax relief. In addition, if a deceased shareholder has a surviving spouse, it is typically desirable to have the deceased's shares "vested indefeasibly" in the surviving spouse or, if a spousal trust is created, in the spousal trust. To "vest indefeasibly" means that the spouse acquiring the shares obtains a right to absolute ownership of the shares such that the right cannot be taken away by any future event.

Under the *Income Tax Act* (Canada), assets are transferred to a spouse on a tax-deferred basis, unless the executor of the deceased elects out of this provision.

Upon the death of a shareholder, one tax strategy is to elect out of the deferred spousal transfer up to the amount of the capital gain exemption available to the deceased shareholder. This allows for a bumped up adjusted cost base of the shares being transferred to the spouse and no tax consequence to the deceased shareholder. The surviving spouse in turn can utilize the capital gain exemption that is available to him or her. In effect, there is a doubling up on the capital gains exemption on these shares.

In order to effect this plan, however, the USA must include the provision for the deceased shareholder's shares to vest indefeasibly to their surviving spouse. The spouse or spousal trust must receive the shares free of any obligation to sell. It is important therefore that the USA acknowledge the right of the deceased to transfer shares to the spouse or spousal trust provided that the spouse or spousal trust becomes a party to the shareholder agreement. The USA would then give the spouse or spousal trust a "put" right (the right of the spouse to require a purchase of the shares by either the surviving shareholders, the corporation, or a combination of the shareholders and the corporation in the proportions determined by the spouse or spousal trust). If the surviving spouse does not exercise the "put" right, the surviving shareholders would then have a "call" right (an option to purchase or to cause the corporation to purchase the remaining shares held by the spouse or spousal trust). The result is that the spouse or spousal trust acquires the shares before any mandatory sale obligation is triggered. Through its prior right to exercise the put option, the spouse or spousal trust has first choice on the way in which the purchase of the shares is affected. The various share purchase options are discussed in the next chapter. If, however, the spouse or spousal trust does not exercise that first choice, the surviving shareholders may choose how the purchase of the shares is affected.

Disability and Critical Illness

A prime objective of most shareholder agreements is certainty. Therefore, there will often be a strong desire to define when the buy-sell provision operates in the case of disability. For example, the provision might kick in if the shareholder is unable to work for six consecutive months. However, a seven-month disability is not necessarily a "permanent" one.

There are several definitions for the word *permanent* for which the words "continuing indefinitely without change" are included. More specifically, the *Black Law Dictionary*, fifth edition, 1979 defines "permanent disability" to mean, among other things:

"Incapacity forever from returning to work formerly performed before accident, though this incapacity may be either total or partial."

Several CRA and government discussions around permanent disability seem to involve a disability that has incapacitated the individual from performing functions formerly performed before the event that caused the disability and there is no reason to believe that such incapacity will not continue throughout the lifetime of the person.

Another more practical approach may also be considered, which is the use of the terms and definitions as provided by the insurance company that is funding the disability buy-out. The proceeds will not be received unless the shareholder's disability falls within the definition of the insurance company.

The waiting period should also be defined, for example, one year from the onset of the disability.

Unlike the death of a shareholder, disability funding, typically an insurance product, does not populate the capital dividend account; therefore, it is not paid tax-free to the disabled shareholder. The proceeds are tax-free to the corporation; however, when paid to the shareholder the amount is taxable. Shareholders have two options for disability funding.

Personally held disability insurance. The premiums are paid by the shareholder and the company may increase compensation to allow for premium payments. The increased compensation is taxable to the shareholder.
Increase in the amount of disability payout to compensate for taxes. The net payment after tax, to the shareholder would be the same as a tax-free amount. In this case, the company pays for the disability premium.

Using "critical illness" to initiate a "triggering event" is not recommended, because it is possible to recover from a critical illness in a short period of time. For example, a shareholder may have a heart attack and recover or have been successfully treated for cancer. In both cases, the trigger to sell shares of the company would be inappropriate.

Critical illness insurance does not populate the capital dividend account; therefore, it is not paid tax-free to the shareholder.

As at death, a disabled shareholder's objective is to maximize the after-tax proceeds of his/her equity for the benefit of the heirs. However, the disabled shareholder may have to expend the funds over his/her lifetime in order to fund living expenses while still having the ability to provide for his/her family after death. These costs, both during the shareholder's lifetime and after death, can be significant as the cash requirement could be substantial.

There are a number of ways to deal with the cash requirements of a disabled shareholder. One of the best methods is the use of other people's money in the form of disability or critical illness insurance for the shareholder. The potential impact on the business must also be considered to determine whether the company will require access to cash in the event that a shareholder becomes disabled. The way in which the period of disability will be funded will also be dependent on the time that the person is disabled. Both disability and critical illness can be long-term or short-term; short-term, long-term, and permanent disabilities should be treated differently in the agreement. Triggering events for critical illness should be separate and apart from the definition of disability. They are distinctly different in nature both from a health perspective as well as a triggering event for USA purposes.

Disagreement

Matters arising between shareholders are frequently the cause of significant dispute and recrimination. The objective and the result of a well-drafted shareholder agreement should be to reduce the play of emotion, and to allow reason and an objective evaluation of the monetary cost to drive the actions taken. Consider including the following:

Dispute Resolution: How to resolve deadlocks amongst shareholders can be resolved. A common mechanism in a shareholder agreement is to limit the dispute resolution process to mediation or binding arbitration which is a considerably less expensive alternative than seeking restitution through the courts.

Unanimous Shareholder Approval: A shareholder agreement can set out a class of material decisions which require unanimous shareholder approval. If the company has a majority shareholder this clause is important to ensure that he/she is not able to make unilateral decisions without first obtaining the consent of all shareholders involved.

Share Transfer: To protect all shareholders, a shareholder's agreement typically contains a primary rule that no shares be transferred without prior approval of the directors. The following mechanisms are designed to protect all shareholder interests and can be used either alone or in combination.

- **Right of First Refusal:** A shareholder who receives an offer from a third party to purchase his/her shares must first allow the existing shareholders the right to match such offer prior to selling to any third party. Without this mechanism, remaining shareholders would not have the option to purchase the shares from the selling shareholder. This protects the shareholders from a third party exercising control over the corporation in the future.

- **Buy-Sell or "Shot Gun" Provision:** This provision allows one shareholder to offer the other shareholders a price and establish the terms under which he/she is prepared to either purchase the other shareholder's interests or sell his/her interest to the other shareholders. The other shareholders then have the option to decide whether they wish to either buy the offered shares or sell their own shares on the same terms and conditions presented. This provision can be very useful in the event of a shareholder dispute where the relationship between the shareholders has broken down and one party wishes to exit.

Compulsory Obligation: A mandatory provision stating upon a specified event the shareholders are obligated to buy-sell the shares at a predetermined price.

Divorce

In order to prevent shares from being transferred to incompatible "partners" such as the spouse of a shareholder as a result of a marital breakdown, consider the inclusion of provisions to give the remaining shareholders the entitlement to buy out the shareholder undergoing division of property and/or that shareholder's spouse. A "call" right is often employed in these circumstances and directions should include price determination, and whether the right is limited to the shares sought to be ordered to be transferred to the spouse.

Issues arising from a marital breakdown of a shareholder are:

- The business interest may be an asset subject to the division of property rules under provincial matrimonial laws.
- The laws may require the shareholder to provide an amount equal to a portion of his/her business interest or even of the actual business interest itself to his/her former spouse.
- The result may be the addition of an additional shareholder or a significant debt upon the shareholder because of the division of assets. Their dividend and other business policies may no longer align with the other shareholders.

Retirement

Retirement differs from death, disability, divorce, disagreement, and critical illness because it is usually a factor of age and is, or should be, a planned event. As such, it should come as no surprise to the other shareholders and therefore should not present too great an adverse impact on the corporation. Although retirement is usually prepared for in advance and is often discussed and resolved by the shareholders outside of their buy-sell agreement, it should be addressed in the shareholder agreement covering issues such as continued holding of shares, valuation of the shares, payment terms for buy-out, non-competition clauses, and post-retirement consulting.

In situations where the shareholders are contemplating succession among themselves or an involved family member, provisions allowing for a smooth transition of ownership should be included in the agreement.

Share Valuation

The various triggers of a USA revolve around when and how much a shareholder will receive at a trigger date.

When a shareholder dies, he/she is deemed immediately before his/her death to have disposed of his/her shares and to have received fair market value for those shares. The issue arises when fair market value is either higher or lower than the formula set out in the USA as the purchase price for the shares.

Canada Revenue Agency's position on valuation in a USA is that the USA must represent a bona fide business arrangement among shareholders as though they were dealing at an arm's length basis, adding that the agreement must not be a "device to pass the descendant's shares to his/her heirs for less than an adequate and full consideration."

Although life insurance proceeds may be used to assist

in purchasing the deceased's shares, it is important that the USA clearly define that the life insurance proceeds do not increase the fair market value of the corporation for buy-sell purposes. It is important, however, to note that the cash surrender value of a life insurance policy is considered an asset of the corporation and as such, the cash surrender value will be considered an asset when determining the value of the corporate shares.

Another consideration regarding the funding of buy-sell agreements is the size of the life insurance benefits compared to the funding needs. Consideration should be given to addressing the potential funding discrepancy on death.

The determination of value has been the cause of many disputes. To mitigate this issue, a well-thought-out valuation clause is important. The basis of the valuation of the company should be discussed among the shareholders, and a reference to who should perform the valuation should be included in the agreement. More specifically, a Chartered Business Valuator or perhaps two should perform separate valuations and the midpoint between the two will be the agreed upon amount. More often than not, business owners believe that their accountant is qualified to perform the valuation. However, it is rare that a general accounting practitioner or a tax specialist has the training and qualification to perform a business valuation. Guidance on how to settle a valuation dispute should be included in the agreement.

When drafting the USA, shareholders should consider the terms from both sides of the equation. What would happen if they were causing the triggering event or if they were buying or responding to the triggering event. The best result is what would be fair and equitable in both events.

Other tax implications to discuss with the drafting lawyer include association rules between corporations and the effect of the USA on the CCPC status of the corporation, both of which are beyond the scope of this book.

In this chapter, we have discussed

- definition of six triggering events of a USA
- criteria to be considered for each triggering event
- need for flexibility in the USA regarding tax changes
- importance of a qualified business valuation
- requirement of payment of through the Capital Dividend Account
- consultation among lawyers, accountants, and insurance advisors
- stop-loss rules and their effect on a USA
- eligible dividends and their effect on a USA

In this chapter, we have discussed the tax savings

For the shareholder:

- buy-sell funding with corporate life insurance using after-tax corporate dollars. Average cost savings is 30 percent.
- life insurance proceeds paid tax-free to the deceased shareholder's estate via the capital dividend account

In Chapter Fifteen–Workbook, you will find additional information

- checklist for Unanimous Shareholders Agreement
- stop-loss rules
- importance of the capital dividend account

Chapter Six

Buy-Sell Funding

Adequate funding for a USA is important for the financial health of the company and its continued success. It provides the remaining shareholders with funds to continue the operations of the business and protects their financial stability. It provides creditors with security and knowledge that the company can continue to meet its financial obligations.

There are several factors that determine the type of buy-sell funding that should be adopted:

- the power of the corporation to purchase its own shares
- the number of shareholders
- flexibility for planning corporate control after the buy-sell transaction
- funding considerations
- Family Law considerations

A USA is not complete unless it has determined the funding method of the buy-sell agreement at any trigger date. There are four types of funding:

1. **Holy cow what do I do now method.** Basically, no preparation and the company scrambles to fund the buy-sell agreement.
2. **Bank financing.** This is often considered the most probable solution. However, it is important to consider the position that the bank is in. If one of the key members of the business is unable to work or has passed away, this could potentially negatively impact the company's bottom line. Banks are usually reluctant to lend money in these situations. Further, in these circumstances when a loan also currently exists, banks have been known to call the loan, rather than consider additional financing.
3. **Self-funding is also an option.** The company creates and builds a fund to ensure that there are adequate funds as needed. If a company has a long-time horizon during which it can build up this pot of money, this could be a good option. Reality, however, is that no one knows exactly when they are going to die or become disabled. In the event of an untimely death, the accumulated funds may not be adequate. Another consideration regarding self-funding the buy-sell is that as the corporation builds up its fund, the investment income earned is considered passive income and will be taxed at between 44.67 percent and 50.67 percent, depending on your province of residence. The result is that a good portion of the growth is eroded through taxes. In addition,

depending on the corporate structure, the fund could also be subject to corporate creditors. If the fund is held in the holding company, creditor issues are less of a concern. In addition, if the fund is held at the operating company level, then the company may not qualify as a Qualified Small Business Corporation resulting in the shares not being deemed eligible for the Enhanced Capital Gains Exemption. The result is the loss of up to $800,000 (2014) of tax-free capital gains for each of the shareholders.

4. **Life insurance or the use of other people's money is a cost-effective way to fund a buy-sell agreement on the death of a shareholder.** Typically, life insurance costs are pennies on the dollar. In addition, if there is a premature death, the funds are available immediately. That is, the corporation does not have to build up a fund, which can take years. The life insurance proceeds are tax-free to the corporation and the funds flow to the deceased shareholder's estate via the capital dividend account.

The type of buy-sell funding chosen should be clearly stated in the buy-sell agreement. If life insurance is used as a funding vehicle, it is important the agreement include the following:

- identify the owner, beneficiary, and premium payor of the insurance policy
- identify the insurance policies on a schedule that is separate from the agreement and update it as necessary
- limit the assignments of the insurance policies, that is the use of the policies as collateral for personal loans
- use of the capital dividend account for share redemptions
- allow for the purchase of the insurance policies on termination of the USA

Four Buy-Sell Ownership Structures

- Criss-Cross Buy-Sell Structure
- Share Redemption Buy-Sell Structure
- Promissory Note Buy-Sell Structure
- Hybrid Buy-Sell Structure

Criss-Cross Buy-Sell Structure

The criss-cross buy-sell transaction at trigger date occurs at the shareholder level. The deceased or departing shareholder sells his shares to the surviving shareholder or shareholders. Although Lucy has not yet sold any WestCoast shares, throughout this chapter, we will use "George" for illustration purposes as WestCoast's new shareholder. Based on this hypothetical scenario, he would own 30 percent of WestCoast.

For example, in Lucy's situation, should George predecease Lucy, under the criss-cross buy-sell structure, Lucy would be required to purchase George's shares at the value as determined by the agreement.

The USA binds George's estate to sell his interest to the surviving shareholder, Lucy.

Lucy owns, is the beneficiary, and pays for George's life insurance policy that she has purchased to fund the buy-sell agreement, and vice versa. Upon George's death, therefore, George's life insurance proceeds are paid directly to Lucy and she uses the funds to purchase George's shares from his estate.

The steps are as follows:

1. The buy-sell agreement states that the surviving shareholder is to purchase the deceased shareholder's shares.
2. The deceased shareholder can take advantage of the capital gains exemption ($800,000 in 2014) if corporate shares are Qualified Small Business Corporation (QSBC) shares, mitigating date-of-death taxes.
3. The surviving shareholder gets a bumped-up Adjusted Cost Base on his/her shares of the company based on the purchase price of the deceased shareholder's shares.

As a result of the criss-cross method, George's estate was able to utilize the capital gains exemption on the sale of his shares to Lucy, up to the maximum available to him at that time.

Lucy would then become the sole shareholder of the corporation. She has increased the number of shares she owns by the number of shares purchased from George's estate. In addition, Lucy would be able to get a bump up in the adjusted cost base of her new shares purchased from George's estate. This eliminates the possibility of double taxation when she passes away or sells her shares.

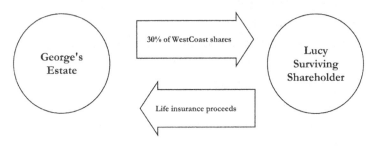

Benefits of a Criss-Cross Buy-Sell Structure

- It is a simple structure when less than four shareholders.
- The corporation does not get involved in the transaction; everything is done at the shareholder level.
- Life insurance proceeds provide surviving shareholders with funds to implement the buy-sell agreement.
- The deceased's estate gets timely receipt of funds.
- It allows the deceased shareholder to take advantage of the capital gains exemption ($800,000 in 2014) if corporate shares are Qualified Small Business Corporation (QSBC) shares, providing tax relief at death.
- The surviving shareholders have the flexibility of adjusting the percentage ownership of the company through allocation of shares of the deceased.

- The surviving shareholder gets a bumped-up Adjusted Cost Base on his/her shares of the company based on the purchase price of the deceased shareholder's shares.

Drawbacks of a Criss-Cross Buy-Sell Structure

- The insurance costs are paid with after-tax personal dollars.
- Age, health, and ownership percentage impact the insurance cost of the various shareholders. The result could be an inequity in the cost of insurance for the shareholders.
- This process relies on each shareholder to maintain his/her personal life insurance funding.
- Multiple shareholders create complexity and difficulty in managing the structure.

Share Redemption Buy-Sell Structure

The share redemption buy-sell transaction at trigger date occurs at the corporate level. The corporation redeems the deceased shareholder's shares at the value determined by the buy-sell agreement. Life insurance is owned by the corporation. The corporation pays the premiums with after-tax corporate dollars, a discount of approximately 30 percent depending on your province of residence. The life insurance premiums are not tax deductible to the corporation.

The steps are as follows:

1. The buy-sell agreement states that the corporation is to redeem the deceased, George's shares.
2. The share redemption results in a deemed dividend. Because the USA includes the use of the capital dividend account when life insurance proceeds are received, the payment to George's estate is tax-free via the capital dividend account.

As a result of the share redemption method, George's estate would be able to receive the proceeds of the share redemption tax-free via the capital dividend account. If the life insurance proceeds are less than the fair market value of the shares at time of death, any dividends paid to the estate over the amount of the life insurance proceeds received will be taxable to the estate, because the capital dividend account's value is based on the life insurance proceeds received.

Lucy is now the sole shareholder of the corporation. The share redemption method does not result in an increase in the cost base of Lucy's shares even though the value of her shares have increased by virtue of the redemption of George's shares. The result is double taxation when Lucy disposes of the shares. In effect, although Lucy has not increased the number of WestCoast shares she owns, they now carry 100 percent of the value of WestCoast compared to 70 percent prior to George's death.

The USA During the Lifetime of the Shareholders

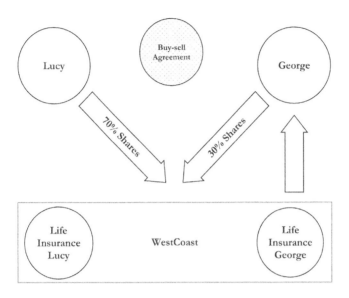

Upon George's Death as Shareholder

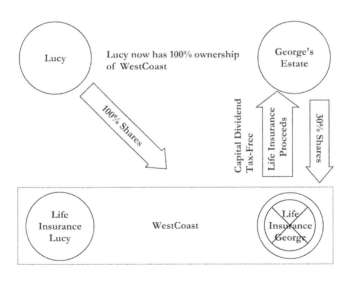

Benefits of a Share Redemption Buy-Sell Structure

- It is a relatively simple to structure with more than three employees.
- Life insurance proceeds provide the company with funds to implement the buy-sell agreement.
- The deceased's estate gets timely receipt of funds.
- It provides tax-free life insurance proceeds via the capital dividend account.
- If stop-loss rules apply, income tax is deferred on first death.
- Insurance premiums are paid with after-tax corporate dollars.
- Insurance premium costs are proportionate to the shareholders' ownerships.

Drawbacks of a Promissory Note Buy-Sell Structure

- The deceased shareholder will not be able to utilize the enhanced capital gains exemption.
- Surviving shareholder does not have an increase in the Adjusted Cost Base of the shares.
- Life insurance proceeds are subject to corporate creditors.
- The corporate solvency test has to be met prior to the declaration of a dividend.

Promissory Note Buy-Sell Structure

The promissory note buy-sell transaction at trigger date occurs at both the corporate and shareholder level. Life insurance is held in the corporation and proceeds flow out of the corporation on a tax-free basis to fund the buy-sell structure.

The steps are as follows:

1. The buy-sell agreement states that the surviving shareholder, Lucy, is to purchase the shares of the deceased, George. A promissory note is drawn by Lucy for the amount owing to George's estate.
2. At this point, Lucy is the sole shareholder, and a capital dividend is declared on the shares in the amount of the life insurance proceeds.
3. Lucy receives the life insurance proceeds tax-free and pays off the promissory note owing to George's estate.

As a result of the promissory note method, George's estate is able to maximize his available capital gains exemption as well as receive the balance of the life insurance proceeds in a time efficient manner.

Lucy is now the sole shareholder of the corporation. She is able to receive a bump up in the adjusted cost base of the shares she purchased from George's estate, eliminating double taxation.

Step 1 of the Buy-Sell Agreement

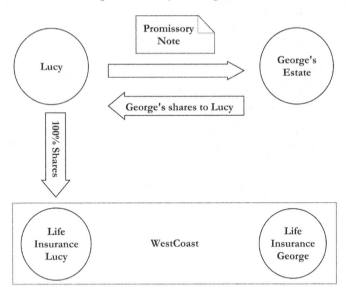

Step 2 of the Buy-Sell Agreement

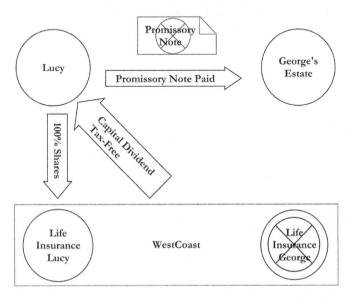

Benefits of a Promissory Note Buy-Sell Structure

- It is relatively simple to structure, establish, and administer.
- Life insurance proceeds provide the surviving shareholders with funds to implement the buy-sell agreement.
- The deceased's estate gets timely receipt of funds.
- The deceased shareholder can take full advantage of the capital gains exemption ($800,000 in 2014) if the company shares are QSBC shares.
- The surviving shareholder gets a bump up of the adjusted cost base of newly acquired shares.
- It provides for the payment of tax-free life insurance proceeds via the capital dividend account, initially to the deceased's estate and then to the surviving shareholder to extinguish the promissory note payable to the deceased's estate.
- Insurance premiums are paid with after-tax corporate dollars.
- Insurance premium costs are proportionate to the shareholders' ownerships.

Drawbacks of a Promissory Note Buy-Sell Structure

- Life insurance proceeds are subject to corporate creditors.
- If proceeds are over the capital gain exemption available to the deceased shareholder, capital gains tax is payable.
- The corporate solvency test has to be met prior to the declaration of a dividend.

Hybrid Buy-Sell Structure

The hybrid buy-sell transaction is the most flexible buy-sell structure. It allows tax planning to occur at trigger date, resulting in the maximization of the available capital gains exemption of the deceased shareholder as well as utilizing the capital dividend account for tax-free proceeds. As a result, at trigger date both the corporation and shareholder are involved in the buy-sell buyout. As with the share redemption and promissory note structure, life insurance is owned and paid by the corporation.

The steps are as follows:

1. The buy-sell agreement states that the surviving shareholder, Lucy, is to purchase the shares of the deceased, George, up to the maximum capital gain exemption available to him. A promissory note is drawn by Lucy for the amount owing to George's estate.
2. The balance of the shares are then redeemed by the corporation and a portion of the life insurance proceeds are used to pay for these shares. The funds flow to George's estate tax-free via the capital dividend account.
3. At this point, Lucy is the sole shareholder and a capital dividend is declared on the shares for the balance of the life insurance proceeds. Lucy receives the life insurance proceeds tax-free and pays off the promissory note owing to George's estate.

As a result of the hybrid method, George's estate is able to maximize his available capital gains exemption as well as receive proceeds tax-free via the capital dividend account.

Lucy is now the sole shareholder of the corporation. She is able to receive a bump up in the adjusted cost base of the shares she purchased from George's estate, minimizing double taxation.

Step 1 of the Hybrid Buy-Sell Structure

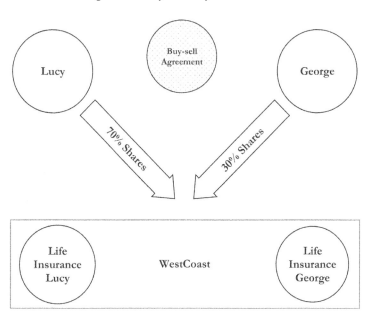

Step 2 of the Hybrid Buy-Sell Structure

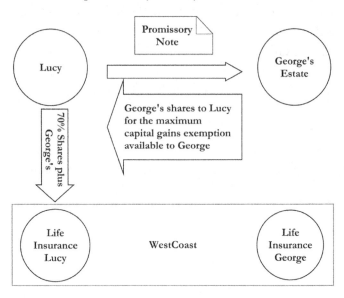

Step 3 of the Hybrid Buy-Sell Structure

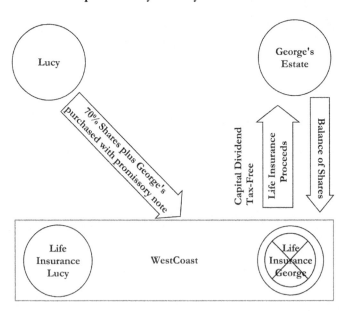

Step 4 of the Hybrid Buy-Sell Structure

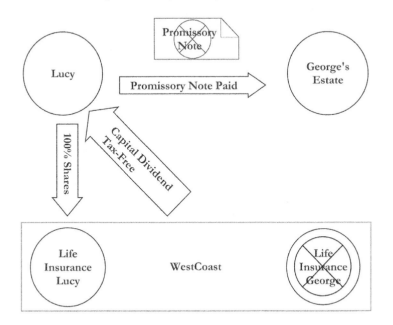

Benefits of a Hybrid Buy-Sell Structure

- It is a relatively simple structure to establish and administer.
- Life insurance proceeds provide the surviving shareholders with funds to implement the buy-sell agreement.
- The deceased's estate gets timely receipt of funds.
- The deceased shareholder can take full advantage of the capital gains exemption ($800,000 in 2014) if the company shares are QSBC shares.
- The surviving shareholder gets a bump up of the adjusted cost base of newly acquired shares.
- Tax-free life insurance proceeds are paid to the estate via the capital dividend account.
- Insurance premiums are paid with after-tax corporate dollars.
- Insurance premium costs are proportionate to the shareholders' ownership.

Drawbacks of a Hybrid Buy-Sell Structure

- Life insurance proceeds are subject to corporate creditors.
- There is no bump up of the adjusted cost base of the shares redeemed by the corporation.
- The corporate solvency test has to be met prior to the declaration of a dividend.

Corporate Versus Personally Owned Life Insurance to Fund Buy-Sell Agreements

Of the four buy-sell structures listed above, only the criss-cross buy-sell structure uses personally held life insurance. The rest of the structures include corporately held life insurance. If it is imperative that each shareholder own their own life insurance, the choice of what type of buy-sell structure to implement is made for you: specifically, the criss-cross method.

Benefits of Corporate Life Insurance

Cost savings—Generally, life insurance premiums are a non-deductible expense for income tax purposes. However, using after-tax corporate funds is desirable, especially when the corporate tax rate is lower than the shareholders' tax rates. This factor alone makes the decision of corporate-owned insurance favourable.

Policy premiums—To keep a life insurance policy in force, the premiums must be paid on a timely basis. Where the insurance is personally owned, it may be difficult for the shareholders to ensure the others are continuing to make the necessary policy premium payments. When the corporation owns the policies, each shareholder has access to corporate records to ensure that the policies are being kept in force.

Cost of insurance premiums—Where there is a difference in age or health between the various shareholders, personal ownership of the life insurance policies places a heavy premium burden on the other shareholders. When the corporation owns the policies and pays the premiums, the cost of each policy is shared among the shareholders according to their pro rata interest in the company. Many shareholders find this a more equitable costing method.

Administration—The criss-cross method is really only feasible from an administrative perspective when there are three or fewer shareholders. After that, it becomes an administrative nightmare. Corporate-owned insurance requires that there be only one insurance policy per shareholder making it much easier to administer.

Family law—It is important to review and understand the family law issues relating to your province of residence. For example, in Ontario, where a corporation owns life insurance policies on the lives of its shareholders, the death benefit loses its character as "life insurance proceeds" when flowed out to the shareholders to fund the buy-sell agreement. As a consequence, the value of the surviving shareholders' net family property will increase, ultimately increasing the equalization claim that could be made by the shareholder's spouse under the *Family Law Act*. It may, therefore, be more beneficial to have life insurance owned personally to reduce potential claims under the *Family Law Act*.

Tax complexity—Corporate-owned life insurance is more complicated from a tax perspective. Although the proceeds of a life insurance policy are tax-free to the corporation, capital dividends must be declared to pass the proceeds to the deceased's estate on a tax-free basis. In addition, depending on the circumstances, all of the proceeds may not be tax-free. Tax considerations include the stop-loss rules, limiting the loss carry-back to the deceased's estate to a maximum of 50 percent. Stop-loss rules are discussed in greater detail in Chapter Fifteen–Workbook.

Creditor protection—The proceeds of a corporate-owned life insurance policy that is paid into the operating company will be subject to the claims of the corporate creditors. In addition, lending institutions can place restrictions on the company's ability to pay dividends to shareholders before their loan is repaid. The result is that the surviving shareholders will not be able to fulfill the terms of their buy-sell agreement. One important planning tool for shareholders is to have individual holding companies to hold their life insurance policies, among other investments. Tax-free intercorporate dividends can be used to fund the policy premiums, and lending institution restrictions will be eliminated.

Once the type of buy-sell agreement is determined and it has been agreed to fund the buy-sell agreement with life insurance, the following are common structural problems:

- There is a mismatch between the buy-sell method and the ownership and beneficiary designation of the life insurance policies.
- When using corporate life insurance funding and when there are steps at both the shareholder and corporate level, it is important to ensure the steps are described in the agreement and in the proper sequence to execute the agreement.

Use of Holding Companies as Owners of Buy-Sell Life Insurance

Another consideration that should be given is the use of holding companies to own the life insurance policies for buy-sell funding purposes. There are several reasons for this ownership structure:

- The life insurance premiums are still funded with after-tax corporate dollars.
- The life insurance policy does not have to be transferred when it is no longer needed by the corporation for buy-sell funding.
- The beneficiary can still be the operating company; more specifically the operating company can be named as an irrevocable beneficiary. The importance of the "irrevocable beneficiary" election is so that the shareholder cannot change the beneficiary at any point in time. All shareholders will have to agree to the change.

- The beneficiary, upon unanimous agreement can be changed to each shareholder's respective holding company if there are any creditor issues.

In this chapter, we have discussed

- four different buy-sell funding structures:
  1. criss-cross buy-sell structure
  2. share redemption buy-sell structure
  3. promissory note buy-sell structure
  4. hybrid buy-sell structure
- four different buy-sell funding options
- benefits and drawbacks of each of the four different buy-sell structures
- information about what documentation is required to be included in life insurance funded buy-sell agreements
- common structural problems of life-insurance-funded buy-sell agreements
- corporate versus personally owned life insurance for buy-sell funding
- use of holding companies as owners of buy-sell life insurance

In Chapter Fifteen–Workbook, you will find additional information

- stop-loss rules
- importance of the capital dividend account

Chapter Seven

Employee Retention

Through the whole process of preparing WestCoast for expansion and a new shareholder, Lucy became aware of the positive impact and importance that Zoey plays in the day-to-day operations of the company. Although Zoey finds her job challenging and feels she is being compensated adequately, Lucy is looking for a creative way to ensure that Zoey will stay with WestCoast for a long time into the future. Lucy, therefore, approached us to see if there were any employee-retention strategies that she could initiate. Lucy also mentioned that she could foresee Zoey in some kind of equity position at some point in the future.

Some of the employee-retention strategies offered to Lucy:

- Wage Loss Replacement Plan
- Individual Pension Plan
- Phantom Stock Options

Lucy was already aware of the **Wage Loss Replacement Plan (WLRP)** strategy and feels that it is worth pursuing for Zoey. The Wage Loss Replacement Plan is an insurance program that provides a greater degree of coverage than a traditional group disability program can offer. Unlike group disability insurance programs, the WLRP is made up of individual disability insurance policies grouped together under a common plan. The plan must have two or more employees. The employer is typically the owner and pays the premiums for the individual contracts. The employees are the insured and benefits are paid directly to them in case of disability. The benefits of this plan are that the premiums are tax deductible to WestCoast, and there is no taxable employee benefit for the premiums paid on the employees' behalves. Any disability income received by the employee is taxable.

While Lucy feels that the **Individual Pension Plan (IPP)** is not suitable for Zoey at this time, she is very intrigued and wanted more information about the Phantom Stock Options. Further information about IPPs is available in Chapter 15 – Workbook.

The idea behind **Phantom Stock Options** is to motivate employees to look beyond current year earnings. They empower employees to make a difference in the growth of the company and take part in that growth from an earnings perspective. The plan mimics equity participation in a company without the company having to issue shares. This plan allows the shareholders to view their management team as business partners rather than employees.

The phantom plan is flexible without interfering with an existing corporate equity structure. Because no stock is actually issued, a phantom stock plan does not dilute the corporation's equity. Instead, payments out of the plan reduce corporate profits. Because actual shares are not involved, taxation to the employee occurs on receipt of the amount paid under the plan and the employer is entitled to a deduction equal to the amount of the payment made to the employee.

Another positive factor is that the phantom plan

typically does not vest until retirement, change of control, or termination of employment and, therefore, provides a true long-term link between the key employee and the corporation. The value of the entitlement of a participant under a phantom plan is directly correlated to the share value of the corporation, although it does not involve the actual ownership of shares. Participants are typically issued "phantom units," the value of which is pegged to the current fair market value of the corporation's shares.

Typically, after certain prescribed conditions are met, the units vest and the employee(s) is entitled to a cash payment equal to the value of the units.

The prescribed conditions vary widely between companies because they are personalized to each corporation, but they are commonly based upon the passage of a certain amount of time and the attainment of performance criteria.

Forfeiture provisions are also a common feature of phantom stock options. Once the phantom units mature and the agreed-upon amount is paid to the employee and reported in his or her income in the year the amount is received, a deduction for that amount may be claimed by the corporation.

In 1991, the Department of Finance Canada introduced paragraph 6801(d) of the Income Tax Regulations to allow special tax treatment for phantom stocks where those plans meet the following conditions:

- Payment is made after retirement, termination of employment, or death ("the triggering events").
- The payment must be made before the end of the calendar year following the one in which any of the triggering events occurred.

- The amount of the payment must be determined on the basis of the fair market value of the shares of the employer corporation within one year of the occurrence of a triggering event.
- There can be no guaranteed minimum payment.

The amount received by the employee under this type of plan will be taxed to the employee as employment income in the year the funds are received from the plan. If the plan doesn't meet these conditions, the employee would be taxed when entitlement to the payment occurred, rather than when the actual payment was received. The result could be punitive from a tax perspective. The employee would not have received the income, but would still have to pay the taxes on the entitlement yet to be received.

In all cases, it is necessary to ensure that an employee's entitlement under a phantom plan is contingent upon one or more factors in order to avoid unfavourable treatment by Canada Revenue Agency.

A phantom plan should, therefore, require that the amount receivable be contingent on factors such as:

- continued employment with the corporation for a fixed number of years,
- the attainment by the corporation of a fixed amount of growth, or
- some other incentive feature.

In the absence of any such conditions, the amounts granted to an employee under a phantom plan will be included in the income of that employee, rendering the employee liable for tax on the amount.

The phantom stock plans also have several tax advantages that are attractive to business owners and key employees:

- The key employee receives share rights under a company's phantom stock program. Canada Revenue Agency does not recognize that receipt as taxable income to the employee until they receive the money.
- Although on receipt of the funds, the payment is treated as employment income in the hands of the recipient, the employee benefits from the deferral of tax on the increase in value of the company shares.
- The company is entitled to a full deduction for the payment made for the phantom plan.

It is important that the phantom stock plan is correctly executed or adverse tax consequences as described above will result. It is important, therefore, that a lawyer complete the agreement to ensure all terms and conditions meet Canada Revenue Agency's requirements.

Lucy sees that the phantom stock purchase plan could provide Zoey with many of the benefits of equity participation without WestCoast having the complications of equity dilution and regular corporate valuations. She sees this plan as a win for WestCoast and a win for Zoey.

In this chapter, we have discussed

Employee-retention strategies:

- Wage Loss Replacement Plan
- Phantom Stock Program

In this chapter, we have discussed these tax savings

For the corporation:

- Wage Loss Replacement Plan—Premiums are fully deductible to the corporation.
- Phantom Stock Plan—Full tax deduction to the corporation occurs upon payment of benefits to the employee.

For the employee:

- Wage Loss Replacement Plan—Premiums are non-taxable benefits.
- Phantom Stock Plan—Although the employee has entitlement under the Phantom Stock Plan, it is not until he/she is paid that taxes are payable.

In Chapter Fifteen–Workbook you will find additional information

- individual pension plans

Chapter Eight

Wealth and Retirement Planning

Wealth and retirement planning for Lucy and Stan is incorporated throughout this book. In this chapter we will review the retirement income generated as a result of Lucy's corporate restructuring. Her retirement planning goes beyond the traditional Registered Retirement Savings Plan. They include:

1. rental income earned by BuildCo,
2. systematic redemption of Lucy's WestCoast freeze-preferred shares,
3. an individual pension plan for Lucy,
4. the mortgage: changing the mindset,
5. split-dollar critical illness return of premiums, and
6. tax-efficient corporate investments for HoldCo.

1. Rental Income Earned by BuildCo

The land and buildings that house WestCoast's head office and manufacturing plant generate rental income. This income is distributed to the trust beneficiaries as needed. If Lucy needs to supplement her retirement income, she has access to regular payments generated by the rental income via the family trust. If the rental income is not needed to supplement Lucy's retirement, BuildCo can reinvest the net income as it sees fit.

2. Systematic Redemption of Lucy's WestCoast Freeze-Preferred Shares

At the time of the corporate restructuring, Lucy was given preferred shares of WestCoast in exchange for her common shares. These shares have a set redemption amount and Lucy will systematically redeem the shares over the course of her retirement.

3. An Individual Pension Plan for Lucy

Another piece of the restructuring plan was to establish a Business Owners Defined Benefit Pension Plan, better known as an Individual Pension Plan (IPP). The IPP provides Lucy with a guaranteed income for life for as long as the IPP is active. The IPP is creditor-protected and the amount of contribution limits are much higher than allowed by an RRSP because it is a defined benefit plan and the funds have to meet the needs of the benefit defined at retirement. In addition, Lucy has the option of past service contributions, which essentially allow her to fund the IPP as if it had been in existence when she founded WestCoast. The only stipulation is that Lucy had to have received a salary in addition to any dividends as income in those years. If she has made contributions to her RRSP over the years, there will be a Past Service Pension Adjustment to the IPP.

All IPP contributions made by WestCoast, the set up fees, and the maintenance fees are fully tax deductible to the corporation. The contributions to the IPP are treated as non-taxable benefits to Lucy. In addition, should WestCoast borrow money to top up Lucy's IPP, the interest is also fully tax deductible. RRSP loans do not have this benefit.

Another benefit of the IPP is that if the business continues after Lucy and Stan pass away and one or both of their sons take over the business, they can be added as members of Lucy's IPP plan. By leaving the plan intact, any assets not used to provide benefits to either Lucy or Stan will remain in the IPP and are transferred to Matt and or Joe without triggering tax.

4. The Mortgage: Changing the Mindset

Although Stan and Lucy generate an above-average family income, they both often wonder where their money goes. Stan would like to see their mortgage paid down quickly so that they can use the freed-up funds to invest for the future. They were presented with another option. It required Stan and Lucy to shift their attitude toward their home and accompanying mortgage. While the home typically increases in value, the gain isn't realized until the sale of the home. Is the home really an asset? Does the home make money or cost money? Homes are rarely assets until they are sold, a new place purchased (at a lower price than the first), and the profit reinvested. In reality, life does not work this way for most people. After some discussion, Stan and Lucy are open to an option that will allow them to pay off their mortgage within a similar time period, build an investment asset that will create an income stream for their retirement, and have insurance for estate planning purposes. All this using the same cash flow as their monthly mortgage payments.

The details of the plan affecting the Parkes' home mortgage are as follows:

- a mortgage balance of $300,000
- $665.15 biweekly mortgage payments
- an amortization period of 25 years

However, with a change in mindset toward their mortgage, the Parkes can achieve the following:

- mortgage paid off in twenty-four and a half years
- $200,000 per person of fully paid permanent life insurance
- $217,000 cash asset available in year twenty-five if the plan is collapsed
- annual income of $8,000 starting when Stan reaches the age of sixty-seven if the plan continues

Our objectives in reframing the Parkes' mortgage outlook:

- to convert non-deductible debt to tax deductible debt
- to build an investment portfolio
- to build an additional income stream during retirement
- to have the mortgage paid off within a similar time period
- to use a similar cash flow as the existing mortgage payment

The result is total debt elimination in twenty-four and a half years and a $217,000 investment portfolio at year twenty-five. This investment portfolio is estimated to produce approximately $8,000 of income annually for Lucy and Stan's retirements.

The drawbacks of the mortgage freedom plan:

- The tax-deductible mortgage is subject to variable mortgage rates.
- The investment component does have market risk, though very limited. The suggested investment portfolio is made up of 80 percent tax-sheltered account and 20 percent public stocks.

5. Split-Dollar Critical-Illness Return of Premiums

To protect WestCoast should Lucy have a critical illness, WestCoast did purchase a critical illness policy with a return-of-premium feature.

It is possible to make payments to a critical illness policy and never make a claim. The good news would be that Lucy is healthy and did not make a claim. In this structure, if there were a claim, WestCoast would receive the proceeds tax-free and could use the funds as it sees fit. In the event there is no claim, Lucy is entitled to receive all premiums paid, tax-free to her personally. This policy provides the option of shared ownership of the critical illness insurance policy, critical illness insurance with return of the premiums paid. This involves Lucy and WestCoast, where they jointly purchase a critical illness policy and enter into a formal "splitting" of rights agreement, including the return of premium payment if no claim is made. The agreement specifies the ownership of each interest more specifically the right to the proceeds in event of claim or the right to the return of premium upon surrender of the policy, their rights, payment of benefits, obligations, and the allocation of the cost of the policy for each party.

WestCoast and Lucy share ownership of a critical illness policy with the return of premium benefit. The corporation will own and pay the premiums for the health insurance benefit while Lucy will own and pay the premiums for the return of premium benefit. Lucy is the insured. If she has a covered critical illness, WestCoast will get the health insurance benefit. If Lucy remains healthy and she is going to retire, WestCoast can cancel coverage, and Lucy will receive a return of all the premiums paid by both WestCoast and Lucy.

This provides critical illness coverage when Lucy and WestCoast need it the most. Once she retires, WestCoast can cancel the coverage and if the policy has been in force for over fifteen years, Lucy will receive all the premiums paid for the policy tax-free. This will provide Lucy with additional capital for her retirement.

6. Tax-Efficient Corporate Investments for HoldCo

Lucy can transfer, via tax-free intercorporate dividends, after-tax profits to her holding company, HoldCo and then invest the funds in tax-sheltered investments. Lucy has approximately 30 percent more funds to invest in HoldCo using after-tax WestCoast dollars than she would have had had she taken the income and invested it personally.

There are several tax efficient vehicles that Lucy can invest in:

- corporate class mutual funds
- bond share arrangements
- exchange-traded funds
- life insurance

Corporate Class Mutual Funds

Ignoring any bias for or against a mutual fund, a corporate class mutual fund can provide significant tax efficiency in a growth market.

There are two significant attributes of the Corporate Class Mutual Funds:

1. tax-free switching
2. reduced taxable distributions

1. Tax-free switching between funds

Through a corporate class mutual fund, you can switch between corporate class mutual funds of the same "umbrella" or company, with no tax cost to the investor. This is possible because each fund is a class of shares in a single mutual fund corporation.

Typically, as you make investment decisions and move your investment to and from various funds, you would be creating taxable dispositions and incurring a tax liability. Within the Corporate Class Mutual Fund structure, however, an investor is able to defer taxes until such time that a withdrawal is made from the fund resulting in a true taxable disposition.

As long as you invest within the funds of the corporate class funds umbrella, taxes on gains are deferred.

When units of the corporate class mutual fund are eventually sold, capital gains are realized and taxable – just like any other investment.

2. Reduced taxable distributions

Compared to standard mutual fund trusts, corporate class mutual funds provide an opportunity to pay less tax on income earned inside a fund.

Gains incurred by all the funds under the corporate class umbrella are able to reduce the taxable exposure to the investor by offsetting losses or expenses from other corporate class funds under the same umbrella. This integration can reduce the taxable distributions the investor receives.

However, like most things in life, there is always a catch.

As already stated the growth is not tax-free; the switch is tax free, but at withdrawal time, the investor will realize the full taxable gain.

In addition, during a down market (for example 2007), if a switch is transacted that results in a capital loss, the loss does not flow to the investor. Alternatively, segregated funds (funds managed through an insurance company), taxable income, and capital losses do flow to the investor, allowing them to decide how to maximize the tax losses.

Bond Share Arrangements

A bond share arrangement is a single investment that

incorporates the benefits of bonds and shares to take advantage of their different tax treatments.

Investing in a bond provides a predetermined static interest rate paid to the bondholder. The interest income is fully taxable to the investor.

Investing in a corporate stock provides the investor with an equity position in the corporation. The shareholder is paid according to the performance of the stock. The investor is taxed on the annual dividend distribution and when the stock is sold, he/she is taxed on the appreciation of the stock, considered a capital gain. Fifty percent of the capital gain is taxable to the investor.

For example, if Lucy were to invest $50,000 of HoldCo's cash in a corporate bond that is paying 8 percent annual interest, HoldCo would receive $4,000 of interest income annually. As interest income, it is fully taxable to HoldCo. Because HoldCo has purchased this corporate bond, Lucy, as shareholder, has the right to purchase shares of the corporation at a nominal value, say $5. Lucy can choose to purchase the shares personally. She will recognize a benefit in approximately five years as the corporate shares increase in value.

In five years, the investment will have accomplished the following:

- earned $20,000 in interest income in HoldCo, resulting in an annual tax bill of $1,827 for a total of $9,134 in the five years (at the 44.67 percent passive tax rate. The passive tax rate ranges between 44.67 and 50.67 percent depending on your province of residence). In turn, the interest income generates a refundable dividend tax on hand (RDTOH) balance for HoldCo, which results in a $1 refund to HoldCo for every $3 of dividends paid to shareholders. RDTOH is one of the vehicles that results in tax integration for Canadian taxpayers.

- increased in value of the $5 corporate shares held by Lucy personally to $20,000. This increase in value is directly related to the positive performance of the company. While an increase of this type is not uncommon, it is not guaranteed. Lucy could invest the $5 and the shares could conceivably drop to a value of zero. If Lucy were to sell her shares, she would be subject to capital gains tax on 50 percent of the increase of $19,995 ($20,000 less $5). At a 44 percent tax rate (Saskatchewan), Lucy incurs a tax liability of $4,399. In effect, Lucy is able to use a corporate asset (the corporate bond) to purchase shares personally at a nominal value and receive a net after-tax amount of $15,596 in her hands.

Exchange-Traded Funds

An exchange-traded fund (ETF) is an investment fund traded on stock exchanges, much like equity stocks. An ETF holds assets such as stocks, commodities, or bonds, and it trades close to its net asset value over the course of the trading day. Most ETFs track an index, such as a stock index or bond index. ETFs are popular options for some investors and certainly have made the investment retail space take notice since 2010. The objective of this book is to look at tax leakage and find tax efficiencies that Stan and Lucy can employ, the merit of a specific product or solution is left to their advisor.

ETFs are not tax efficient in themselves: they are no different from a passively managed mutual fund. They are not tax-sheltered, nor do they offer any specific tax advantage in distributions. If they are owned within a corporate class investment, however, they will enjoy the benefits of tax-free switching as described with the Corporate Class Mutual Funds above.

What makes ETFs attractive to investors is their low management fee and low turnover. The low turnover is achieved since the ETF is usually based on an index of funds such as the S&P 500 Index. Any investment with low turnover will have reduced distributions and, therefore, reduced taxation to the investor.

Life Insurance

Lucy believed that life insurance was solely for the purpose of providing for dependents should she or Stan pass away prematurely, or perhaps for estate tax needs. She was intrigued to learn about another component of life insurance. Life insurance can be used as an investment vehicle and it is especially tax efficient in a corporate setting. Assets generating income that are not used in the active business operations are subject to a higher rate of income tax, ranging from 44.67 percent to 50.67 percent depending on your province of residence (2014). There is substantial tax erosion on any income earned and this increases the timeline when trying to accumulate wealth. The funds invested in the life insurance policy grow tax-deferred, eliminating tax erosion.

Lucy plans to use the assets accumulated within the life insurance policy to supplement her retirement income.

She has the option of triggering a systematic withdrawal of funds to supplement her retirement income or of using the cash value accumulated within the policy as collateral for a personal loan.

It is important to note that the investments in HoldCo should not focus on only one type of investment but rather that the investment portfolio be properly diversified.

Lucy's wealth accumulation and retirement planning has gone beyond the standard Registered Retirement Savings Plans and investment portfolios, and includes the benefits available to business owners with the correct corporate structure to take advantage of the benefits of tax deferral and deductions available to them.

In this chapter, we have discussed

The various retirement income sources available to Lucy:

- rental income earned by BuildCo
- systematic redemption of Lucy's WestCoast freeze-preferred shares
- an individual pension plan for Lucy
- the mortgage: changing the mindset
- split-dollar critical illness return of premiums
- tax-efficient corporate investments for HoldCo

In Chapter Fifteen–Workbook, you will find additional information

- individual pension plans

Chapter Nine

Estate Planning

It is important to understand that estate planning extends beyond the estate freeze that Lucy and Stan have implemented. There are many more issues that need to be discussed and considered including the concepts of estate equalization and will planning. In addition to planning around financial issues, it is important to also discuss the family dynamics and how they may play out upon the death of the second parent. With these issues in mind, it is important to have a multidisciplinary group of advisors, such as tax accountants, lawyers, financial advisors, insurance specialists, and family counsellors available to meet all the estate planning needs and goals.

Lucy and Stan's objectives are paramount in achieving a workable personalized estate plan.

Lucy and Stan are planning to continue working for the next ten to fifteen years. Their needs are different from a couple in their mid-sixties who are planning to retire within the next year or two. It is important, however, regardless of the client's age to understand the relationship between the parents and the children before the start of the estate planning process. Although it is not the case with Lucy and Stan, additional issues regarding second marriages, spouses, and children may also need to be addressed.

Once the personal side of the equation has been reviewed and understood, then it is important to gather business information.

Here are some of the key questions:

- What is the current fair market value of the corporation? This provides the information to calculate date-of-death tax liabilities on the corporate shares, if no tax planning has been done such as a restructuring including a family trust.
- What are the current and anticipated cash flow requirements?
- What are the current sources of cash flow?
- What other assets outside the business do Lucy and Stan hold?
- What are Lucy and Stan's current outlook on WestCoast's business and future?

The freeze-preferred shares are only a portion of retirement funding for the typical business owner. Another concern is how will their estate fund their date-of-death tax liabilities? The current result of Lucy's estate freeze is that she is able to determine her date-of-death tax liability from a business perspective based on her fixed value freeze-preferred shares. Any future growth of WestCoast is attributed to the shares held by the Parke Family Trust. Because Lucy's tax liability for her business shares is fixed, her estate plan can include planning for the funding specifically for this tax liability. An affordable solution may be the purchase of permanent life insurance to cover this tax liability. We do not know when Lucy will die and it may be very likely that she systematically redeems her freeze shares to fund a portion of her retirement. The result is that with each share redemption, her date-of-death tax liability decreases, because she is paying the relevant taxes with each redemption.

The economic viability of WestCoast is very important, because Lucy and Stan need to determine if it can meet their current and future cash flow requirements taking into account any retirement funding that Stan has accumulated through his work life.

Once this information has been assembled and discussed, Lucy and Stan can begin to determine the objectives of their estate plan.

Key objectives for many business owners include

Tax Minimization

The freeze-preferred shares have fixed Lucy's date-of-death tax liability for her business assets. In addition, probate fees are decreased since only her freeze shares will be in probate. Lucy controls the balance of her corporate assets, but she does not own them and; therefore, there are no date-of-death taxes or probate fees attributable to them.

Date-of-Death Tax Liabilities

The freeze allows Lucy to start planning how her estate will pay for her tax liabilities. She has many options including systematic share redemption (time permitting), charitable giving, or life insurance.

Financial Security

Lucy is in control of her financial security while she works at WestCoast. What happens when she relinquishes control? Will she be better off selling her business? Consideration must be given to ensure cash flow needs will be met.

Retention of Control

Retention of control for Lucy at this time is crucial. Upon retirement, it is her plan to have a successor in place to protect her investment in the company. This may include the sale of her business to a third party, depending on the career choices of her sons. Both or neither may want to work in and/or run the company.

Flexibility

A family trust is a wonderful tool that preserves flexibility when planning for the future. It is impossible to plan with full knowledge of what will happen in the future, but the family trust will protect against as many unknowns as possible.

The creation of the Parke Family Trust has provided Lucy and Stan with a very powerful planning tool. The primary benefit of the trust is to allow future growth in WestCoast to accrue for the benefit of the trust beneficiaries without having to predetermine the allocation of that growth until some later time, when the trust assets are distributed on a tax-free basis to the beneficiaries. Another benefit is the ability to enhanced income-splitting opportunities for the family. Should Matt and/or Joe plan a career around

WestCoast, they will be able to participate in the profits of the company through dividend payments via the family trust. As Lucy determines each son's potential future at WestCoast, she can transfer WestCoast shares to them at the Trust's cost base. This is achieved through a capital distribution of the trust. At the time of transfer, future tax savings can be achieved through capital gains exemption planning.

Fair Treatment of Family Members

Currently Lucy does not know whether either of her two sons is interested in developing his career at WestCoast. Her estate plan, however, must at least contemplate the possibly of either son or only one son remaining in the business. This objective takes on more importance if both decide not to participate in the business.

Maximization of Enhanced Capital Gains Exemption

It is important for all business owners to maximize and multiply the enhanced capital gains exemption. HoldCo has been created to facilitate the "purification" of WestCoast to ensure that it maintains its "qualified small business corporation" status.

Creditor Proofing

Creditor proofing may be an important requirement of the estate plan or an opportune side benefit of the freeze. Creditor proofing for Lucy and Stan has involved the creation of HoldCo, BuildCo, and a family trust. When assets are transferred to another entity such as a holding company, creditor protection is only available if the transfer is done in good faith and not in anticipation of a creditor or legal issue.

Income Splitting

The family trust has generated income and capital splitting opportunities for Lucy with Stan and their children, as they reach the age of majority. In a few years, Matt will be attending post-secondary education. Once he attains the age of eighteen, he will be able to receive approximately $25,000 of annual tax-free income from the family trust. (Manitoba and Prince Edward Island are exceptions, with approximately $15,000.) The actual amount depends on his province of residence. This is a tax-efficient way to fund Matt and Joe's post-secondary educations.

Probate Planning

In many provinces, probate fees are expensive. In others, such as Alberta, the maximum probate fee is $400. In British Columbia by contrast, the probate fees are 1.4 percent of the fair market value of the estate over $50,000. From an estate perspective, once probate fees have been estimated, some planning can be done to mitigate the cost.

To avoid paying probate fees, many individuals transfer their assets into joint ownership. This is a popular estate planning strategy, but it is important to understand the consequences of the transfer to determine if it is the correct strategy for you and your estate plan. Although minimizing tax and estate administration costs may be the purpose of joint ownership, the risks and outcomes may outweigh any tax savings.

Two or more parties who own property together hold the property in joint tenancy. Each joint owner has rights of use, control, access, and income allocation in respect to the property.

It is important to be aware of the court's treatment of property held jointly by parents and children. The *Pecore v. Pecore* case (2007 SCC 17) is a harsh reminder that parents should not add a child's name to bank accounts or other property without proper legal advice. In the Pecore case, the Supreme Court of Canada acknowledged that there are legitimate reasons why parents transfer property into joint names with children, including assisting with financial management, simplifying estate administration, and avoiding probate fees payable on death. But what is important is how the balance of the asset is treated. Does it make up part of the estate, or was that asset intended to be for the sole use of the joint owner? When the intentions of the parent's transfer is unclear, legal issues arise. It is, therefore, strongly advisable to set a letter of intention for the asset or assets that are transferred into joint ownership so that all heirs and the courts understand how the asset is to be treated upon the death of the parent.

Chapter Twelve – Joint Ownership discusses this topic in full detail.

Apart from the more complex planning that we have discussed regarding Lucy and Stan's estate plan, it is also important to ensure that the following documents are in order:

Will

Perhaps the most critical and most commonly misunderstood legal document in the estate planning process is the Will. It is the cornerstone upon which all estate planning is based, and it is also the reference point for all other personal planning decisions.

The Will determines who will receive the assets owned by the testator on the date of death.

In the absence of a Will, provincial rules of succession are applied to distribute the estate. While generally running along family lines, these rigid rules can result in unintended inclusion or exclusion of beneficiaries, and often result in substantial financial court and tax costs that would otherwise not have been incurred. In addition, a large portion of the estate can be eroded as a result of not being able to do any tax planning. For example, if Lucy were to predecease Stan, typically all her assets would transfer to Stan. Upon Stan's death, the final tax liability based on his assets would be determined. Without a will, the succession rules divide the estate among the surviving spouse and children. The potential is tax erosion on assets. If the children are minors, then the province "manages" the assets until such time that they reach the age of majority and can manage the assets themselves. Stan can apply to the province to manage the children's assets, but will have to incur legal and court costs to do so.

Power of Attorney

A Power of Attorney is an opportunity for you (the "donor") to share decision-making powers over your financial and/or personal affairs with another person, called your "attorney." By executing a Power of Attorney you do not lose your own ability to make those decisions.

A Power of Attorney can be viewed as an extension of yourself. By choosing a trusted person and providing adequate instructions, you can ensure that your wealth and wellbeing are maintained when you are not available to make necessary decisions.

In the unfortunate circumstance that your mental abilities have permanently diminished, the existence of valid Powers of Attorney will ease the emotional burden on your family, and avoid or substantially reduce the cost, complexity, and time delays that may be associated with a court application for your guardianship.

Power of Attorney for Property

This enables your attorney to make decisions regarding your finances, personal property, and real estate. Subject to the restrictions you define, your attorney will be able to do anything you can do with your property, except execute a Will or effect testamentary dispositions such as changes to insurance beneficiary designations.

Personal Health Care Directive

This enables your attorney to make decisions related to your personal wellbeing, including health care, nutrition, shelter, clothing, hygiene, and safety.

It is, however, not enough to execute these documents and put them in a drawer, or worst, in a safe deposit box where no one can access them. The documents should be in a place where anyone can access them in case of need.

Even though a Will, a Power of Attorney, and a personal health care directive are the most frequently created documents, a list of passwords and logins for everything is also invaluable. In addition, creating a list of the companies and services that direct-debit from your bank accounts and of your credit cards is a must so that they can be contacted and the services stopped or payments continued as required. For example, an elderly man's children closed a bank account to stop all direct debit payments. What they did not realize was that a $1 million insurance policy was being paid out of this account. The result was that the policy was terminated for non-payment.

And, last but not least, don't forget the mundane things like how the house alarm works, the sprinkler system, the key to the mailbox. Prepare a list as if you were renting it to someone for the summer and needed to leave instructions. Every little bit helps.

In this chapter, we have discussed

- gathering information to start an estate plan
- the objectives of estate planning
- the importance of a will, powers of attorney and health care directives

In Chapter Fifteen–Workbook, you will find additional information

- will questionnaire
- power of attorney questionnaire
- personal health care directive questionnaire

Chapter Ten

Risk Management

Life is unpredictable. Unforeseen events can sometimes wreak havoc on the best-laid plans. Managing risk is a major element of Lucy and Stan's financial plan.

Insurance products are excellent tools to help deal with life's uncertainties and protect their lifestyle and their family and business.

Lucy and Stan focus on these risk-management goals:

- protecting Lucy and Stan's ability to earn an income
- protecting Lucy's investment in her business
- protecting the family
- protecting retirement assets

They need these types of risk coverage:

- life insurance for Stan and Lucy's income replacement
- life insurance for mortgage payout
- long-term disability insurance for Lucy; Stan is covered by his employer
- independent living for Lucy and Stan
- critical illness insurance for Lucy
- health and travel insurances for the family

Lucy and Stan will need to determine their overall threshold for the amount of risk they are willing to cover and how much they actually need.

From a personal perspective, they consider this insurance coverage:

- life insurance for Stan's income replacement—a term 20 policy (a twenty-year life insurance policy) would cover his salary until retirement.
- life insurance for mortgage buyout—discussion of this is included in the Mortgage: Changing the Mindset as discussed in Chapter Eight, which includes a life insurance component.
- independent living for Lucy and Stan. They are still young so the cost for coverage will be substantially less to buy now than if they were to buy it upon retirement. The other issue is health. They are both currently insurable.
- travel insurance for the family

From a business perspective, they consider this insurance coverage:

- life insurance—permanent for buy-sell funding purposes
- life insurance for wealth management and estate planning
- long-term disability insurance with a Wage Loss Replacement Plan
- split-dollar critical illness insurance for Lucy
- health insurance covered through WestCoast with a Private Health Services Plan

The new corporate structure has provided Lucy and Stan with the flexibility of wealth and retirement planning using tax-deferred funds. Their holding company HoldCo is being used extensively in their planning. Lucy is able to move after-tax corporate dollars from WestCoast to HoldCo on a tax-free basis via intercorporate dividends. This process will allow Lucy to transfer excess cash out of WestCoast, maintaining WestCoast's "qualified small business corporation" status for the capital gains exemption, as well as to defer taxes and invest the funds for wealth accumulation and retirement planning.

Corporate Life Insurance

We have determined that there are two different needs for life insurance: buy-sell funding, and wealth accumulation and retirement planning. Neither of the two policies are tax deductible for the corporation. The insurance policy for the buy-sell funding requirements will be a separate policy. In addition, a joint last-to-die universal life insurance policy will be purchased to accommodate wealth accumulation and retirement planning. Because Lucy is using after-tax corporate dollars to pay for the insurance policies, she is enjoying approximately 30 percent in cost savings, the difference between her tax rate and the low small business tax rate.

The buy-sell funding policy will be a whole life policy with paid-up additions. In effect, this is a lifelong policy; the paid-up additions—the income earned by the policy—are reinvested into the policy through the purchase of additional life insurance. This will provide coverage for Lucy's buy-sell needs. However, should the company be sold and buy-sell funding no longer be required, the whole life policy can become part of Lucy's retirement and/or estate plan. As time passes, the paid-up additions increase the value of the policy. This provides additional coverage as the company value increases. It most likely will not keep up with WestCoast's growth, but it will increase in value nonetheless. HoldCo will be the owner of the policy and WestCoast the irrevocable beneficiary. As the irrevocable beneficiary, WestCoast directors will be notified of any beneficiary changes or lapse in premium payments. It is a safety net to ensure the buy-sell funding is maintained by the shareholders and the proceeds flow to WestCoast to meet the buy-sell requirements. If WestCoast is sold prior to Lucy's death, the beneficiary can be changed to HoldCo with no tax consequence.

One of the retirement and wealth accumulation vehicles is a joint last-to-die universal life insurance policy. Joint last-to-die is a policy on both Lucy and Stan's lives, and it pays out when the second spouse dies. Life insurance can also be used as an investment vehicle that accumulates assets in a tax-sheltered environment. It provides life-long insurance coverage and includes a savings component. The universal life insurance policy allows for the deposit of cash for investments that are managed by the owner of the policy. As long as the investments are in the universal life policy, any growth is tax deferred. Over time, the policy builds a cash-surrender value. This is considered an asset by lenders, and can be used to collateralize a personal loan in the future or to supplement retirement income. A word of caution: If the cash-surrender value of the corporation's life insurance is used as collateral for a personal loan, it is important that the shareholder, Lucy, pay the company for the use of this asset. The payment is called a "guarantor" fee. Canada Revenue Agency has opined that the guarantor fee should be the difference between the interest rate the individual would have been charged by the bank without the collateral and the interest rate being charged with the collateral. Best practice dictates that if there is no difference, then the current Canada Revenue Agency prescribed rate be applied to the collateralized loan amount and be paid to the corporation (in 2014 the prescribed rate is 1 percent). Documentation should always be kept to support the amount being paid. Lucy will make regular deposits into the universal life policy for investment purposes.

Life insurance proceeds are tax-free proceeds to the corporation. They are paid to the estate of the deceased shareholder on a tax-free basis via the capital dividend account. The Capital Dividend Account is a fundamental tax-planning tool for private Canadian corporations and their shareholders; public corporations do not qualify for this treatment.

Taxation in Canada is based on the fundamental tax principle of integration. Under this principle, individuals receive life insurance proceeds tax-free. Corporations afford the same tax treatment of tax-free life insurance proceeds. The issue, therefore, is how do shareholders receive the tax-free life insurance proceeds? The mechanism set out by Canada Revenue Agency is the capital dividend account. It is a notional account that is created to track tax-free receipts of a private corporation that may be distributed as tax-free capital dividends to its shareholders.

Wage Loss Replacement Plan

A Wage Loss Replacement Plan (WLRP) is an insurance program that offers a more comprehensive disability coverage than a group disability program can offer. It is put in place by the employer to provide disability income protection for a specific group of employees. It need not be for all employees of the company, but rather for a group that falls within a defined class, such as management or professional employees.

Lucy, the new shareholder, and her management team will be included in the WLRP. The result is that Lucy will receive a more comprehensive disability plan that is tax deductible to the corporation, and the plan premiums are not taxable to Lucy or the other employees also receiving this plan. The payments, if claimed, are paid directly to the employee. The company is not involved.

A WLRP is converting what would normally be a personal expense for the employee into a tax-deductible expense for the business.

Critical Illness Policy

A critical illness policy provides a tax-free lump sum cash payment upon diagnosis of a range of covered critical illnesses such as heart attack, cancer, and stroke. WestCoast will purchase coverage on Lucy. There are a number of reasons why WestCoast would like Lucy to be covered for a critical illness.

1. **To protect against the loss associated with
   Lucy's sickness**

   If Lucy becomes critically ill, the corporation may
   require funds to meet immediate cash needs and
   to find a replacement during this time of illness.
   Critical illness coverage provides cash to buy time
   for the business and/or to provide funds to hire a
   temporary replacement during Lucy's illness.

2. **To meet corporate obligations arising on Lucy's
   sickness**

   Stand-alone critical illness insurance can provide
   the funding needed to repay business debts in the
   event of Lucy's critical illness because the event of
   a critical illness could result in repayment demands
   of creditors or restrictions on corporate loans.

3. **To provide funding for buy-sell arrangements**

   A shareholders' agreement may provide for the
   purchase and sale of shares of a company in the
   event of a shareholder's critical illness. Many critical illnesses result in full recovery so it is important
   that the terms of the shareholder agreement regarding critical illness are clearly thought through
   as to whether or not the event of a critical illness
   is a "triggering event" and whether it requires a
   mandatory or optional buy-out. There may be a
   waiting period once a critical illness has occurred
   and perhaps the critical illness insurance proceeds

are held for a period and then used as necessary for the triggered buy-out.

Shared Ownership of a Critical Illness Insurance Policy with Return of Premium

If Lucy does become critically ill, WestCoast will receive a lump sum amount of cash.

This provides critical illness coverage when Lucy and WestCoast need it the most. If, however, Lucy does not make a claim for critical illness, once she retires, WestCoast can cancel the coverage and if it is over fifteen years from when the critical illness coverage started, Lucy will receive all the premiums paid for the policy tax-free. Detailed discussion of shared ownership critical illness insurance is in Chapter Eight – Wealth and Retirement Planning.

Private Health Services Plan

A Private Health Services Plan (PHSP) is an effective way for a business to convert all health, medical, and dental expenses to a fully tax-deductible business expense. It is a Canada Revenue Agency approved plan that allows medical expenses of business owners to become a deductible business expense for the company. WestCoast will establish a PHSP for the Parke family. This is a nationwide plan that provides affordable medical coverage for the business owner and his/her family.

A PHSP can result in significant savings for the business owner and his/her family. The cost of the plan is low and there are no monthly premiums, no renewal charges. The plan covers pre-existing medical conditions and 100 percent of the expense is covered, and there is no need for the employee to pay a deductible.

Effectively, this plan allows business owners and their employees to have health costs paid with the business's pre-tax dollars, rather than having them paid with personal tax-paid funds.

In this chapter, we have discussed

- risk management from a personal and business perspective
- risk plans that are paid with after-tax personal dollars
- risk plans that are paid with after-tax corporate dollars

In Chapter Fifteen–Workbook, you will find additional information

- capital dividend account
- risk management

Chapter Eleven

Putting It All Together

We've met the Parkes—Lucy and Stan and their children Matt and Joe—and discussed the growth issues Lucy is facing with her business WestCoast. Lucy's plan is to grow WestCoast to sales of over $5 million, but to do so; she requires additional capital for marketing and a manufacturing expansion. Lucy's main concern is that her family and business planning have not been integrated and, while WestCoast is very important to the Parke family's financial wellbeing, Lucy would like a plan that considers her family as well as her business.

From a business perspective, Lucy would like to increase WestCoast sales and believes bringing in a new shareholder will facilitate the cash requirements as well as provide a complementary skill set to take WestCoast to the next level. But most importantly, Lucy does not want to move forward if these plans will jeopardize the Parke family.

Through several discussions, it became clear that Lucy's first step is to have a corporate structure that will facilitate growth and expansion. Although Stan is no longer directly involved in WestCoast, it is important to Lucy that he be included in her planning. After considerable thought, Lucy and Stan clarified their objectives:

1. to provide a strong foundation for WestCoast's growth, Lucy and Stan's retirement and succession planning. In so doing, Lucy is to be compensated for the equity she has produced in WestCoast to date.
2. to provide an effective strategy through which to transfer ownership of WestCoast
3. to securitize and protect the Parke family's financial position and on a go-forward basis to ensure their lifestyles are guaranteed. This includes claims by creditors and possible future matrimonial breakdown
4. to plan for unanticipated events including long-term disability and premature death
5. to assist with their sons' (Matt and Joe) post-secondary educations in a tax-effective manner
6. to minimize taxes, professional fees, and other costs associated with the ongoing management and ultimate disposition of their estate

Lucy and Stan have implemented many of our suggestions and the following six objectives are the result of their new business, retirement, and estate planning.

1. To provide a strong foundation for WestCoast's growth, Lucy and Stan's retirement and succession planning. In so doing, Lucy is to be compensated for the equity she has produced in WestCoast to date.

As proposed earlier, Lucy has chosen to go forward with a corporate restructuring that includes the creation of a family trust, holding company, and a separate company for the ownership of WestCoast's land and building.

The Result of the Restructuring

Originally, WestCoast's assets included excess cash, a small portfolio of investments, the land, and the buildings that housed WestCoast's head office and manufacturing plant. To protect their assets from creditors' claims, the Parkes transferred these assets into two separate newly created companies. The holding company, HoldCo, now owns the excess cash and investment portfolio that Lucy has amassed over the last few years. HoldCo will lend the excess cash to WestCoast as needed during the upcoming growth phase. In addition, as WestCoast generates additional income, HoldCo is the vehicle through which Lucy will start saving for her retirement and estate-planning purposes, while at the same time ensuring that WestCoast maintains its "qualified small business corporation" status.

This chart illustrates the benefit of tax deferral when Lucy transfers after-tax WestCoast dollars to HoldCo. She has 31 percent more dollars available for investing at the HoldCo level versus paying the money directly to herself, paying personal tax, and then investing the balance.

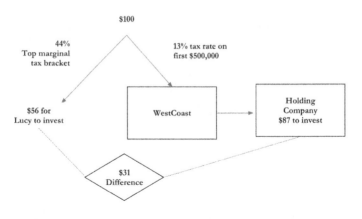

Saskatchewan 2014 tax rates

The building company, BuildCo, now owns the land and buildings that house WestCoast's head office and manufacturing plant.

Segregating these assets from WestCoast meets several of Lucy's objectives:

- creditor protection
- maintaining WestCoast's qualified small business status
- rental income providing additional funds for Lucy's retirement
- tax deferred investing in HoldCo

The creation of the Parke Family Trust provides Lucy with an effective tool for corporate tax and estate planning. Lucy has effectively transferred her WestCoast assets for the benefit of her family, the trust is now the owner of all of WestCoast's growth shares. As a trustee, Lucy controls the assets of the trust, thereby, she effectively controls WestCoast. In addition, the trust provides her with flexibility to decide how and when she will ease out of the business and transfer control. The trust also provides an effective vehicle for income splitting with adult family members.

2. To provide an effective strategy through which to transfer ownership of WestCoast

The trust has the ability to transfer assets to any or all of its beneficiaries at its adjusted cost base. This provides Lucy with the ability to transfer shares of WestCoast to either or both of Matt or Joe should they decide to make WestCoast their career choice. Lucy can choose to transfer the trust's WestCoast shares at their adjusted cost base, which is minimal, or at fair market value.

Should neither Matt nor Joe become part of the WestCoast succession plan, then Lucy, as trustee, can sell the growth shares to the new shareholder. The sale price is at fair market value. The benefit of the trust at this time is the multiplication of access to the $800,000 capital gains exemption.

In effect, there is $2.4 million of tax-free capital gains to take advantage of once both Matt and Joe attain the age of eighteen (2014 figures).

3. To securitize and protect the Parkes' financial position and on a go-forward basis to ensure their lifestyles are guaranteed. This includes claims by creditors and possible future matrimonial breakdown.

HoldCo provides creditor protection through the movement of excess cash from WestCoast to the holding company. Only operating funds and minimal assets are held in WestCoast. It is important, however, to be aware of provincial legislation regarding fraudulent conveyances. Each province's legislation gives "creditors" the right to have conveyances of property set aside if they are done with an intent to hinder them—or, in some cases, if they have the effect of hindering them—in their collection efforts. Specifically, if assets have been fraudulently transferred from an offending company, creditors have access to those funds to meet the company's obligations.

Lucy's restructuring has been created in good faith; more importantly, the transfers were not done with an intent to defeat the claims of existing creditors or contingent creditors; for example, the potential liability regarding guarantees made by WestCoast on their products. As a result, this structure provides the Parke family with creditor protection in many ways.

In the same vein, BuildCo provides creditor protection for the capital assets, specifically for WestCoast's land and buildings.

The Parke Family Trust provides creditor protection because of its status as a fully discretionary trust, specifically; no one beneficiary has ownership of any of the assets. Family law issues are less easy to deal with definitively. However, careful planning leaves control of the corporation in the hands of the operator of the business and may indeed in some circumstances exclude property from the category of shareable matrimonial property. The family law rules are specific to each province so it is important to ensure that proper legal advice is obtained for your province of residence.

4. To plan for unanticipated events, including long-term disability and premature death.

Wage Loss Replacement Plan. Lucy, in her capacity as an employee, has established the Wage Loss Replacement Plan (WLRP) to ensure that she, the new shareholder, and key employees are covered in the event of long-term disability. The WLRP is an insurance program that provides a greater degree of coverage than a traditional group disability program can offer. The benefit of this plan is that the premiums are tax deductible to WestCoast, but there is no employee benefit for the premiums paid on their behalf. The income is paid directly by the insurance company to the employees in the case of a claim.

Split-dollar Critical Illness. Lucy has also purchased a split-dollar critical illness policy to ensure that WestCoast has funds if needed should she have a critical illness. Any new shareholders will also purchase the same type of policy. A critical illness policy provides a tax-free lump-sum cash payment upon diagnosis of a range of covered critical illnesses such as heart attack, cancer, and stroke.

Lucy is aware that it is possible to make payments to a critical illness policy and a claim is never made. The good news is Lucy is healthy and does not make a claim. It is possible for Lucy to receive the premiums she has paid into the policy tax-free if there is no claim made with the purchase of a return of premium rider. Lucy and WestCoast jointly purchase a critical illness policy and enter into a formal "splitting" of rights agreement, including the return of premium payment if no claim is made.

This provides critical illness coverage when Lucy and WestCoast need it the most. Once Lucy retires, WestCoast can cancel the coverage and if it is over fifteen years from when the coverage started, Lucy will receive all of the premiums paid for the policy tax-free, that is both the premiums paid by WestCoast and those paid by Lucy.

Private Health Services Plan. Lucy set up a private health services plan (PHSP) for her family. This plan is an effective way for the business to convert all health, medical, and dental expenses into a fully tax-deductible business expense. This is a nationwide plan that provides affordable medical coverage for the business owner and his/her family. Effectively, this plan allows Lucy to have her family health costs paid with WestCoast's pre-tax dollars, rather than having them paid with her after-tax dollars.

Life Insurance. Lucy has two different needs for life insurance: buy-sell funding and wealth accumulation (retirement and estate planning). Neither of the policy premiums are tax deductible to the corporation; however, Lucy is using after-tax corporate dollars to fund the policies. This affords her approximately a 30 percent cost savings because of the tax rate difference between her top marginal rate and the low small business tax rate.

The buy-sell funding policy is a separate policy that will be used solely to fund the buy-sell agreement. Should the buy-sell agreement end and the coverage no longer required, the policy can be kept in force and used for estate planning purposes or cancelled and the cash value used for retirement purposes.

In addition, a joint last-to-die universal life insurance policy will be purchased to accommodate wealth accumulation and retirement planning.

Joint last-to-die is a policy on both Lucy and Stan's life and it pays out when the second spouse passes away. A universal life insurance policy has two components. The policy coverage, which is the amount of insurance coverage purchased, is being used for estate planning purposes. The second an investment component, and in Lucy's case, she is using that benefit as a tax-sheltered investment vehicle. The policy provides both life-long life insurance coverage and a tax-sheltered investment environment. The investments are managed by the owner of the policy, in this case, Lucy, as shareholder of WestCoast. As long as the investments are in the universal life policy, their growth is tax deferred.

5. To assist with their sons' (Matt and Joe) post-secondary educations in a tax effective manner

The Parke Family Trust has provided Lucy with the ability to fund Matt and Joe's post-secondary educations with after-tax corporate dollars. Dividends are paid to both Matt and Joe (once they are over the age of seventeen) via the family trust. They are able to receive approximately $25,000 of tax-free income annually if they have minimal or no other sources of income.

The chart below illustrates that through income splitting with either Matt or Joe, both of whom are in a lower income tax bracket than either Lucy or Stan, there is a $31 cash flow benefit when compared to paying Lucy $100 at her high tax bracket. (We have used 2014 Saskatchewan tax rates for illustration purposes only.) This is a very effective way to fund post-secondary education for adult children of business owners without giving the children direct ownership of the company .

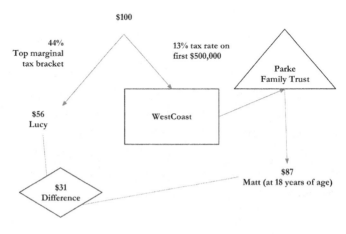

Saskatchewan 2014 tax rates

6. To minimize taxes, professional fees, and other costs associated with the ongoing management and ultimate disposition of their estate

The common shares of WestCoast, Holdco, and BuildCo that are held by the Parke Family Trust are not subject to deemed disposition rules otherwise applicable on any beneficiary's death. (The assets of the trust, however, are subject to the twenty-one year disposition rule. There is tax planning required around the twenty-one year trust rule, which is beyond the scope of this book.) Lucy is subject to the deemed disposition rules only for the value of the preferred shares of WestCoast that she holds at her death. In addition, although Lucy's capital interest in the Parke Family Trust will be deemed to be disposed of at death, she can argue that her interest is worthless because of the discretionary nature of the trust.

The trust can be used to provide creditor protection and to transfer property to Lucy and Stan's heirs without the use of a will. So, if your province of residence has wills variation legislation and high probate fees, neither will affect the transfer of assets from the trust upon the death of either Lucy or Stan. (This is subject to family law considerations in most provinces.)

The trust is not required to register with any government body other than to submit the required annual tax return filings. As a result, the accumulation of assets in the trust is private, so Lucy and Stan have enhanced confidentiality with the use of a trust.

Both Lucy and Stan are satisfied that the corporate restructuring and the tax planning that has occurred provides them with tax savings now and has a positive impact on their wealth accumulation, retirement, and estate planning.

Fast forward thirty years. Lucy and Stan are now seventy-five and seventy-eight respectively. Both Matt and Joe have married and Lucy and Stan have three grandchildren. Joe is now the CEO of WestCoast and Matt has a successful career as the owner of a multimedia technology company.

Stan retired at the age of sixty-five and Lucy at the age of sixty; she handed over the reins of WestCoast to Joe. Because of the corporate restructuring Lucy undertook, she was able to systematically transfer WestCoast shares to Joe as he showed commitment and ability as a strong leader for WestCoast. At retirement, Lucy started redeeming her freeze-preferred shares. These shares have been a part of her retirement income.

Under the original plan, Lucy, in HoldCo, started saving for her retirement in tax-efficient investment vehicles, including a universal life insurance policy. At the time, neither Matt nor Joe were in a position to decide their eventual careers. This life insurance policy will provide funds for Lucy to ensure that, upon the second death of Lucy or Stan, Matt will receive the life insurance proceeds as an equalization payment for the WestCoast shares transferred to Joe. Joe received WestCoast shares upon Lucy's retirement through the family trust at no cost to him except hard work. Yes, he did work for them and he has contributed greatly to WestCoast's growth over the last ten years.

Another source of income for Lucy's retirement is the IPP she established as part of the corporate restructuring.

She started receiving her defined benefit pension payments at the age of sixty. These payments, as with an RRSP, are fully taxable to Lucy. If Lucy predeceases Stan, Stan will continue to receive a reduced amount of pension from the IPP. The balance that remains in the IPP upon the second death of Lucy and Stan will pass directly without tax consequences to Joe's IPP. This tax-free transfer is because Joe, Lucy's son, is an employee of WestCoast. This is a tremendous tax savings, because, if Lucy had RRSP investments (which must be transferred to a Registered Retirement Income Fund (RRIF) at retirement) at the second death of Lucy and Stan, the balance in the RRIF would be fully taxable on the date-of-death tax return. The result is an erosion of the RRIF asset of almost 50 percent to taxes based on your province of residence.

Lucy still enjoys the rental income that is generated from BuildCo and upon her death both Matt and Joe will benefit from the revenue.

Lucy has benefitted from good health and, at retirement, she received the tax-free return of premiums for the critical illness policy. Lucy took the lump-sum and purchased a non-prescribed annuity, a tax-efficient source of income for life. Approximately two-thirds of the income is a return of capital; the balance is taxable as interest income. A portion of the income is used to fund a life insurance policy to replace the capital spent on the purchase of the annuity. The insurance policy's beneficiary is a trust for the benefit of her grandchildren.

The whole life insurance product that was purchased as part of the Mortgage: Changing the Mindset strategy is now earmarked to pay for Lucy and Stan's date-of-death taxes. This is a joint last-to-die policy. Because Lucy and

Stan's wills each stipulate that either will passes to the other (mirror wills), the tax liability will be at the second death of Lucy or Stan. The policy will pay out at that time as well. This minimizes their estate erosion since the date-of-death taxes will be paid with the insurance proceeds and their estate will not have to sell any assets to pay off the tax liability.

Stan has had some medical issues in the past few years, and Lucy is grateful that they had purchased an independent living policy so that Stan is able to remain in their home. His homecare support is funded by this policy.

Lucy and Stan have had an integrated financial and succession plan that has provided them with a tax effective financial path to accomplish their retirement and succession goals. Throughout their wealth accumulation phase and their retirement and succession phase, they leveraged the tax rules available to small business owners in Canada. Lucy and Stan are still enjoying their family dinners every Sunday to catch up with their sons and their careers, their families, and most importantly spend time with their grandchildren.

You can never get lost if you know where you are going.
Unknown

Chapter Twelve

Joint Ownership

Transferring property to joint ownership with beneficiaries is a popular estate planning strategy, but it is important to understand the consequences of the transfer to determine if it is the correct strategy for you and your estate plan. Although minimizing tax and estate administration costs may be the purpose of joint ownership, the risks and outcomes may outweigh any probate savings.

Two or more parties who own property together hold the property in joint tenancy. Each joint owner has rights of use, control, access, and income allocation with respect to the property. The nature of these rights, both during the owner's lifetime and after death, depends on the type of joint ownership. Joint ownership can be either:

- tenancy in common, or
- joint tenancy with right of survivorship.

Tenancy in Common

Tenancy in common exists when two or more parties jointly have title to property such as real estate, a home, bank accounts, etc. Each tenant in common has equal rights of possession, enjoyment, and access to the property regardless of their pro rata interest in the property. Tenants in common each have the right to dispose of their interest in the property, by sale or gift during their lifetime, or through their will at death. If the asset is held at death, the proportionate share will become part of the deceased's estate and will be passed on as part of the will. Probate costs are not avoided.

Joint Tenancy with Right of Survivorship

Joint tenancy with right of survivorship has the following characteristics:

- The property has two or more owners.
- Each joint owner has full access to, use of, and enjoyment of the property.
- No joint owner can exclude the other joint owners from the property.
- Each joint owner has unrestricted interest in the property as a whole.

The primary difference between tenants in common and joint tenancy is the right of survivorship. With a joint tenancy, when a joint tenant dies, his/her interest in the property automatically passes to the surviving joint tenants. The result is that the asset bypasses probate and does not incur probate fees. With tenants in common, upon death of one of the tenants, his/her interest makes up part of his/her estate.

The following risks should be considered before entering into a joint relationship.

Loss of Control

When another individual is added to the title of your house or onto your investment account, you are adding an owner and giving up sole control of the asset. If at some time in the future you want to sell or use your home as collateral or make changes to your investment accounts, the joint owner must agree to your wishes before you can execute your plans. The joint owner has the right to refuse the changes you would like to make as you are now equal owners of this asset.

Exposure to Creditors

Joint ownership results in a legal ownership and, therefore, the asset can be subject to claims from the joint owner's creditors. These claims could significantly impact your interest in the property by reducing its value or forcing a liquidation. If your family member has potential creditor issues or may be involved in a family law matter, you may want to avoid owning property with him or her.

Tax Consequences

When you transfer property, both you and the joint owner run the risk of incurring a tax liability. When you transfer real estate, even to yourself and another person, you may incur a liability to pay Land Transfer Tax. Equally, if you are transferring a portion of an investment portfolio to another individual, a disposition of 50 percent of the investments is deemed to have occurred. If there are any capital gains related to these assets, you, as transferor, will be liable to pay capital gains tax on the disposition. A principal resident is exempt from capital gains tax, so that transfer will be tax-free. It is important to recognize, however, that any increase in value for the 50 percent ownership of the new owner, if the home is not his/her principal residence, will be subject to capital gains tax. It is important to note that the increase in value of the asset starts to accumulate upon the transfer, not upon the death of the transferor.

Estate Conflict

The transfer of property into joint ownership to a beneficiary of your estate may cause conflict upon death and the distribution of assets. When a transfer is made, it is important that the transferor have a "letter of intent" drawn up to clarify the purpose of the transfer and whether or not the residual value of the asset upon his/her death is to make up a portion of his/her estate. The letter of intent will assist the other beneficiaries of the estate and, if required, will assist the courts in acting on your true wishes.

Costs of Transfer

Implementing a joint ownership structure will cost money. There may be certain up-front costs such as Land Transfer Tax, legal and/or accounting fees, or other tax liabilities.

When considering joint ownership, it is important to weigh the benefits of minimized probate taxes and administration costs with the risks involved. Only make a decision when all the benefits and risks have been evaluated.

Because a joint tenant's interest automatically passes to the surviving joint tenants, the asset bypasses the deceased tenant's estate, and is not subject to probate fees. Although the estate and probate fees are bypassed, taxes are still payable on any capital gain that is associated with the deemed disposition of the asset at death. The capital gain will be reported on the deceased's final tax return.

Advantages of Joint Tenancy

- The property bypasses probate at the death of a joint tenant.
- The property bypasses the estate at death allowing for a quick transfer of title.

Disadvantages of Joint Tenancy

- Transfer of title and re-registration constitutes a disposition of the asset for tax purposes and may result in a tax liability.
- Access to and use of the property as a whole now accrues to the new joint tenant. He/she cannot be excluded from the property even if relationships change.
- The property will now remain with the joint tenant at death so the deceased owner has no ability to name a different beneficiary.
- The property is now accessible to the creditors of the new joint tenant.

When considering the transfer of an asset into either tenants in common or joint tenancy, it is important to review the advantages and disadvantages of each transfer prior to executing the transfer.

As mentioned earlier, it is also important to be aware of the court's treatment of property held jointly by parents and children. The *Pecore v. Pecore* case is a harsh reminder that parents should not add a child's name to bank accounts or other property without proper legal advice.

In *Pecore v. Pecore*, the Supreme Court of Canada acknowledged that there are legitimate reasons why parents transfer property into joint names with children including assistance with financial management, simplification of estate administration, and avoidance of probate fees payable on death.

Property held jointly passes "by right of survivorship" meaning that ownership of the property passes to the surviving joint owner. As a result, one questions whether a property owned jointly by a parent and a child was intended to go directly to that child or whether the property was to be shared with the other siblings equally. More often than not a parent, as in *Pecore v. Pecore*, does not make his/her wishes known and it is left up to the courts to determine what his/her true wishes were.

The judgment delivered on *Pecore v. Pecore* was a definitive statement as to how courts must deal with such cases. It is now the law in Canada that whenever a parent gratuitously transfers property into joint names with an adult child, the court will presume that the property so transferred is not intended to pass to such child on the death of the parent, but is intended to form part of the deceased parent's estate to be distributed in accordance with his/her will. If the child/joint owner asserts that the jointly held property was intended to pass to them alone on the death of the parent, the onus is on the child to prove that this was the parent's intention on a balance of probabilities.

Although the assets held jointly are presumed to be distributed as part of one's estate, the value of such assets will continue to be excluded from the estate for probate purposes.

To conclude on the result of *Pecore v. Pecore*, if a parent decides to hold property jointly with a child, he/she must document their intention with respect to this property, either in the will or in a separate document kept with their will.

In this chapter, we have discussed

- the benefits and risks of Joint Ownership of assets
- the *Pecore v. Pecore* case regarding adding children as joint owners
- the difference between Joint Tenancy and Tenancy-in-Common

Chapter Thirteen

Professional Corporations

Professional corporations have access to many of the same tax benefits that small business owners can enjoy. Before incorporation, however, consideration must be given to the restrictions and rules set by the provincial professional body in question. One of the major differences is the restriction of ownership of the professional corporation. Ownership limitations will have some impact on the tax benefits available to the incorporated professional. Each profession, within each province, has regulatory legislation, regulations, and administrative guidelines. Some professionals are not permitted to incorporate by provincial law; therefore, he/she is prohibited from operating within a corporate structure and cannot assign professional income to that corporation. It is imperative, therefore, that prior to incorporation, the professional understand the regulatory legislation, regulations, and administrative guidelines set out by their provincial governing body. For example, it was not until 2009 that Alberta professionals were able to add family members as shareholders of their professional corporation.

Each of the provincial statutory regimes contains its own rules and constraints. The following summarizes some of the standard requirements for professionals incorporating their practices:

- A professional corporation much obtain an operating permit and renew it annually.
- The incorporation documents should restrict the corporation to the practice of the applicable profession in accordance with its enabling statute. Where holding companies are permitted within the corporate structure, ensure they meet any restrictions that may be imposed on them by virtue of the relationship with the professional corporation. Most provinces do not preclude the professional corporation from holding passive investments.
- The directors of the professional corporation must consist of one or more practising members of the profession licensed in that province or jurisdiction.
- Typically, only licensed professionals can own voting shares of the professional corporation.
- A "unanimous shareholders' agreement" (USA) is valid only if all shareholders are licensed members of the profession. Or, if permitted, the shareholder is a professional corporation. In jurisdictions where family members or a trust can be a non-voting shareholder, the USA will not be a valid document.
- Several provinces permit non-voting shares of the professional corporation to be held by a specified range of relatives, such as the professional's spouse and children, a corporation of which the spouse and children are shareholders, and trusts where the

beneficiaries are specified family members. Alberta professional corporations are permitted family trusts as shareholders; however, the beneficiaries of the trust are restricted only to minor children of the professional, and once the last child beneficiary reaches the age of 18, the trust must be dissolved.

- The same confidentiality, ethical standards, and professional conduct standards apply to incorporated professionals and to those who provide their services directly. The members of a professional corporation and the corporation itself are each subject to the professional regulatory body's disciplinary powers.
- The liability of the professional member for negligence, errors, omissions, and malfeasance, among other things, is not affected by the incorporated status of his/her practice. Generally, the effect of the limited liability protection is restricted to the ordinary commercial obligations that do not constitute a liability in the nature of professional liability.
- Names of the professional corporation usually require one to use their name; for example, Dr. X Dental Corporation.
- Individual professionals are typically liable to pay their respective association dues; however the corporation covers the expense.

Once the professional has determined his/her restrictions and is incorporated, the following are advantages of incorporation.

Availability of the Small Business Tax Rate

One of the most important benefits of incorporation is the ability to defer tax by retaining income in the corporation that is subject to the small business tax rate. If, however, the professional requires all of his/her income earned initially, they may find the benefits of future use.

When more than one professional is incorporating and they are associated, if not properly structured, they may have to share the $500,000 income amount subject to the small business tax rate. (All but two provinces have the $500,000 threshold in 2014: Manitoba's threshold is $425,000 and Nova Scotia's is $350,000.)

Availability of the General Corporate Tax Rate

Even if the professional corporation earns over the $500,000 taxable income threshold that is subject to the lower corporate tax rate, the general income tax rate is still below the top marginal personal tax rate of most provinces. Deferring tax is still an option, and the professional is not required to pay him/herself any more income than is required. The tax deferral benefit is due to lower corporate rates and can be enjoyed until income through dividends are distributed to shareholders.

Remuneration Flexibility

The professional can choose either salary or dividends or a mix of both as remuneration. He/she may consider enough salary to allow maximum Registered Retirement Savings Plan (RRSP) contributions or Canada Pension

Plan contributions. Also, having a salary allows flexibility in retirement planning down the road.

Income Splitting

If the regulating professional body allows a spouse and/or adult children to own non-voting shares of the professional corporation, dividends can be declared on their shares. If their marginal tax rate is lower than the professional's, there can be substantial tax savings.

The following diagram highlights the tax savings when income splitting with an individual taxed at a lower rate. There is a 31 percent savings. Using the income-splitting strategy is great for providing funds for your adult children's post-secondary educations. With no other source of income, an adult child can receive approximately $25,000 in tax-free dividends annually. This is a great tax savings to the parent providing the funding for their children's post-secondary education.

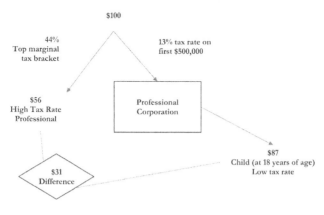

$100

44%
Top marginal
tax bracket

13% tax rate on
first $500,000

$56
High Tax Rate
Professional

Professional
Corporation

$87
Child (at 18 years of age)
Low tax rate

$31
Difference

Saskatchewan 2014 tax rates

Income splitting permits family members who are not active in the practice to receive dividends on shares that they directly or indirectly own. If these family members are eighteen years of age or older, are in a low tax bracket, and the shares are properly issued, then the family as a whole will pay less tax than if the professional had earned all of the income personally.

Access to the $800,000 Capital Gains Exemption

A professional corporation has to meet the same criteria as other corporations to qualify for the $800,000 (2014) capital gains exemption. These criteria are as follows:

- Throughout a period of twenty-four months immediately preceding the trigger date, the corporation's shares must not have been owned by any person or partnership other than the individual who was related to him or her. There is an exemption to this requirement. Shareholders of newly incorporated small business corporations have access to the special exemption of Qualified Small Business Corporation (QSBC) shares even when the corporation has existed for less than twenty-four months. Related to this exemption, a sole proprietor can utilize the capital gains exemption available to the shareholders of qualified shares of a small business corporation by rolling the assets into a newly formed corporation under Section 85 of the Income Tax Act (Canada) and subsequently selling the shares.
- The corporation must be a Canadian Controlled Private Corporation (CCPC). That is, 50 percent

152

or more of the shares must be owned by Canadian residents for tax purposes. Also, the shares must not be traded on the stock exchange.

- Ninety percent or more of the Fair Market Value of the assets of the company must be used in active business at trigger date. Any investments that are not directly required for the day-to-day running of the business are considered passive assets. If the Fair Market Value of these assets is greater than 10 percent, the CCPC will not qualify as a QSBC. Trigger dates are the sale of the business, the death of the shareholder, or restructuring of the company.

- Fifty percent or more of the Fair Market Value of the assets of the company must be used in active business immediately preceding twenty-four months prior to the trigger date.

If the professional regulatory body does not allow another corporation to be a shareholder of the professional corporation, the 90 percent rule might not be met. On the other hand, it is not advisable, from a creditor perspective, to have an excessive amount of assets held within the professional corporation. The creditor protection afforded by Individual Pension Plans is a huge benefit for professionals, which explains their popularity among professionals.

Non-Calendar Year End

All sole proprietors and partnerships are required to have a calendar year end. A professional corporation is not required to do so and has the ability to choose a non-calendar year-end to align with their business cycle.

Payment of Intercorporate Dividends

If the provincial regulatory body permits a corporation to be a shareholder of the professional corporation, then discretionary dividends can be paid by the professional corporation to the holding company. The dividends pass to the holding company tax-free. The funds can then be invested. The benefit is tax deferral; for Saskatchewan in 2014 the deferral is 31 percent.

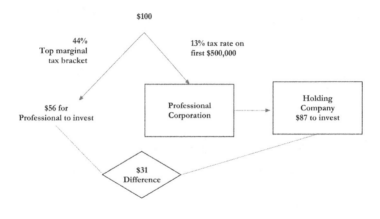

Saskatchewan 2014 tax rates

Investing with the retained earnings of a professional corporation makes excellent sense, because in addition to having more to invest, generally speaking, passive investment income (rent, interest, royalties), capital gains, and portfolio dividends are taxed at virtually the same tax rate regardless of whether the income is earned by a corporation and distributed to a shareholder or earned by the individual directly. This is the theory of tax integration. Because every province has its own tax rate, integration is not a perfect science. When taking into account the ability to use after-tax corporate dollars for investing, the tax deferral and using the holding company to invest allows for more investment dollars and, therefore, a larger investment portfolio, all things being equal.

Asset Protection

The professional does not have limited liability with respect to creditors relating to his/her services. He/she does, however, have limited liability for other liabilities incurred by the professional corporation.

Ability to Establish a Defined Benefit Pension Plan

In recent years, the Individual Pension Plan (IPP) has become an increasingly popular retirement savings option for professionals. IPPs are designed to reach a certain value by the retirement age of the individual in order to provide for a steady income source in retirement. While they are defined benefit pension plans, recognized as Registered Pension Plans (RPPs) by the Canada Revenue Agency, IPPs are designed to provide more pension benefits than are available from traditional vehicles such as RRSPs.

IPPs can only be established by corporations, not by individuals themselves. IPP plan holders must be Canadian residents and must pay Canadian income tax. The plans are often set up for professionals who would like to make higher contributions to a retirement plan than what is currently permitted by the rules governing RRSPs and pension plans. The investments eligible within IPPs are those eligible for use in a defined benefit pension plan, including stocks, investment funds, or Guaranteed Investment Certificates (GIC), as long as no single equity position represents more than 10 percent of the total book value of the plan.

As long as an IPP has been established in good faith by the employer and the employee, the assets will be protected from creditors, making the IPP an attractive alternative for professionals whose professional corporations are not able to have a holding company. The IPP provides another layer of creditor protection.

All IPP contributions, set-up fees, and maintenance fees made by the professional corporation on behalf of the professional are fully tax-deductible to the corporation and treated as a non-taxable benefit to the professional. Interest on funds borrowed by the professional corporation to make IPP contributions are also fully tax-deductible. RRSP loans do not have this benefit.

∽

Ability to Purchase a Shared Ownership of Critical Illness Insurance with Return of Premium

A critical illness policy provides a tax-free lump-sum cash payment upon diagnosis of a range of covered critical illnesses such as heart attack, cancer, and stroke. A professional would consider a stand-alone critical illness policy for many situations including the following:

- protection against the loss associated with the sickness of the professional. If the professional becomes critically ill, the corporation may require funds to meet immediate cash needs and/or to find a replacement during this time of illness.
- to provide funding needed to repay business debts. The critical illness of the professional could result in repayment demands of creditors or restrictions on corporate loans.

Premiums paid for the stand-alone critical illness policy are not tax deductible to the corporation. In turn, the proceeds of a critical illness payout are tax-free to the corporation. It is possible that the professional makes payments to a critical illness policy and a claim is never made. The good news is the professional is healthy and did not make a claim. Professionals, as with business owners, also have access to an option of shared ownership of a critical illness insurance policy, critical illness insurance with return of the premiums paid that returns the premiums paid on the critical illness policy to the shareholder in the event of no claim. The structure involves an agreement between the professional and his/her professional corporation, where they jointly purchase a critical illness policy and enter into a formal "splitting" of rights agreement, including the return of premium payment if no claim is made. The agreement specifies the ownership of each interest, their rights, payment of benefits, obligations, and the allocation of the cost of the policy for each party.

The professional and the corporation share ownership of the critical illness policy with the return of premium benefit. The corporation owns and pays the premiums for the health insurance benefit while the professional will own and pay the premiums for the return of premium benefit. The professional is the insured. If the professional suffers a covered critical illness, the corporation will get the health insurance benefit. If the professional remains healthy, upon retirement (at least fifteen years from purchase of policy) the professional corporation can cancel coverage, and the professional receives a return of all the premiums paid for the stand alone critical illness policy.

Ability to Set Up a Private Health Services Plan

As with an incorporated business, a Private Health Services Plan (PHSP) is also an effective way for an incorporated professional to convert all health, medical, and dental expenses into a fully tax deductible business expense. It is a Canada Revenue Agency approved plan that allows medical expenses of employees and professionals to become a deductible business expense for the professional corporation. This is a nationwide plan that provides affordable medical coverage for the incorporated professional, his/her family, and if they choose, employees.

A PHSP can result in significant savings for the professional and his/her family. The cost of the plan is low and there are no monthly premiums, no renewal charges. The plan covers pre-existing medical conditions and 100 percent of the expense is covered; there is no need for the professional to pay a deductible.

Effectively, this plan allows incorporated professionals and their family to have health costs paid with the corporation's pre-tax dollars, rather than having them paid with personal after-tax funds.

The ability for a professional to incorporate provides the professional with many tax-saving vehicles and opportunities. Each province and each profession is governed by regulations; so before incorporating it is important that the professional seek advice on the regulations governing his or her profession and the rules around incorporation.

In this chapter, we have discussed

- The importance of determining the legislation and regulations relating to the specific professional within their province of residence.
- The benefits of a professional corporation include the following:
  * availability of the small business tax rate
  * availability of the general tax rate
  * remuneration flexibility
  * income splitting
  * access to the $800,000 (2014) capital gains exemption
  * non-calendar year end
  * payment of intercorporate dividends
  * asset protection
  * ability to establish a defined benefit pension plan
  * ability to establish a shared ownership critical illness plan with return of premium
  * ability to set up a private health services plan

In Chapter Fifteen–Workbook, you will find additional information

- personal information gathering
- recording your family genome
- qualified small business corporation status
- individual pension plans
- will questionnaire
- power of attorney questionnaire
- personal health care directive questionnaire
- risk management

Chapter Fourteen

The Business of Farming

I believe that we are born with the desire to farm in our blood. The tradition of family-operated farms is becoming scarcer. The Government of Canada recognizes the importance that the family farm plays in our food production and in our economy. As a result, there are specific tax provisions aimed at the agriculture and fishing industries to trigger financial stimulus. The family farm and family fishing businesses are the only two types of businesses eligible for a tax-deferred transfer to the next generation, regardless of the value of the business. For the remainder of this chapter, the family farm also refers to family fishing.

There are two capital gains tax provisions specifically geared toward farmers and their qualified farm properties, shares of capital stock of a qualified farming business, or interest in a qualified farming partnership:

1. lifetime $800,000 capital gains exemption on the disposition of qualified farm property
2. deferral of income tax on the capital gain from inter-generational farm transfers

Many farms are handed down from one generation to the next. Normally, this transfer of property would trigger a taxable capital gain. However, the intergenerational transfer of farm property defers the taxable capital gain until such time that the farm property is disposed of to a third party, someone outside the family. Specifically, this rollover provision defers the tax on the capital gain of the farm property if the recipient is a child who is farming the property. Farmland, depreciable property, and eligible capital property can be included in the rollover provision.

Farm planning is more difficult than planning for an owner-managed business for the following reasons:

- The family home is typically located within the farm property. Where will the parents live for the remainder of their lives after transferring the management of the farm to their children?
- Retirement income is typically tied up within the farm assets, so it is important to protect the parents' retirement income after transition.
- If some children do not remain active in the farm operations, how does succession treat them without jeopardizing the ongoing viability of the farm operations?
- Proper tax planning is important to eliminate or minimize tax leakage and avoid unnecessary professional fees.

In addition to these unique factors, it is even more important to understand these factors:

- Each farm business is unique.
- Each family has unique aspects and considerations.
- Every succession plan will be unique.

Farm Business Structures

There are three main business structures for operating a farm: sole proprietor, partnership, and corporation.

The following is an overview of the different farm business structures.

Sole Proprietor

- A single farmer operating an unincorporated farming business as a sole owner is considered a "sole proprietor."
- The sole proprietor has equitable ownership of both personal and business assets.
- Business income is also income of a sole owner and is taxed at their personal marginal tax rate.
- A sole proprietor farmer is personally liable for the farm liabilities and his/her personal assets are exposed to the creditors of the farming business.

A sole proprietor has the advantage of ease of establishing the business and minimal administrative aspects; that is, corporate financial statements and tax returns are not required. It is an effective tax structure for the short term, but has limitations for long-term tax and succession planning.

Under the *Income Tax Act* (Canada) (ITA), when a taxpayer transfers property, during their lifetime, to a non-arm's length individual, such as a child, for no proceeds or for less than the fair market value of the asset, the ITA deems the taxpayer to have "sold" the property to that individual at fair market value. This may result in immediate tax consequences to the taxpayer and double taxation when the property is eventually sold. The recipient of the asset transfer has an adjusted cost base of value at which the taxpayer transferred the asset. The result: double taxation.

However, the ITA allows a farmer to transfer farm property to a child on a tax-deferred basis; meaning that the farmer can elect an amount between his/her adjusted cost base and the fair market value of the farm operations at which the asset will transfer to the child.

For succession purposes, farmland, depreciable property such as machinery and buildings, and eligible capital property such as quotas can be transferred by the sole owner to a child on a tax- deferred basis when the following conditions are met according to Subsection 73(3) of the ITA:

a) The property was, immediately before the transfer, land or depreciable property in Canada or eligible capital property in Canada in respect of a farming business carried on in Canada by the taxpayer,

b) The child of the taxpayer was resident in Canada immediately before the transfer, and

c) The property has been used principally in the farming business in which the taxpayer, or the spouse, child, or parent of the taxpayer, was actively engaged on a regular and continuous basis.

It is important to note that farm inventory is not included in the list of tax-deferred assets under the ITA. The potential result is a significant tax burden as the value of the inventory will have to be included in the transferor's tax return in the year of transfer.

When proper succession planning is undertaken, this tax burden can be averted. It is important to plan ahead as many strategies require some time to implement.

Prior to the succession or transfer date, the farmer can transfer his/her farm operations, including depreciable assets, eligible capital property, and inventory into a partnership (of the farmer and his/her spouse) on a tax-deferred basis under the ITA. The partnership must operate as the farming business for at least twenty-four months. After the twenty-four month period, the parents can transfer their interest in the farming partnership, which includes the farm inventory, to the child on a tax-deferred basis.

The ITA provides preferential treatment to farmers on transfers to a child that occur as a result of the farmer's death. Under subsection 70(9) of the ITA, farmland and depreciable farm property can be transferred on a tax-deferred basis if the following conditions are met:

a) The property was, before the death of the taxpayer, land or depreciable property in Canada used principally in the farming business carried on in Canada, which the taxpayer, or the spouse, child, or parent of the taxpayer was actively engaged in on a regular and continuous basis,

b) The child of the taxpayer was resident in Canada immediately before the day on which the taxpayer died, and

c) As a consequence of the taxpayer's death, the property is transferred and becomes indefeasibly vested in the child within thirty-six months from the date of death.

Like qualified small business shares, qualified farm property including, farmland, depreciable property, shares in a qualified farm corporation, or interest in a farm partnership qualify for the lifetime capital gains exemption ($800,000 per individual in 2014). It is important, therefore, to structure any succession plan so that the use of the lifetime capital gains exemption is optimized. For example, upon the transfer of farmland and depreciable property to a child, the farmer can transfer the assets at an amount greater than his/her adjusted cost base (up to the farmer's available lifetime capital gains exemption) and take back, as consideration from the child, promissory notes. These notes can be forgiven through the parents' wills. The result is that the parent has recognized and utilized their capital gains exemption and increased or "bumped up" the adjusted cost base of the farm asset to the child.

The parents may have some Alternative Minimum Tax (AMT) to pay, but essentially the transfer is tax-free. One way to mitigate the AMT on an intergenerational transfer, where the plan involves the use of the capital gains exemption, is to stagger the transfer over a period of years. A reserve can be claimed to spread out the taxation of the capital gain for up to ten years for farm transfers if the following conditions are met:

- The purchaser must be a child of the vendor.
- The capital property disposed of must be land in Canada, depreciable property in Canada, a share of the capital stock of a family farm corporation, or an interest in a family farm partnership.
- Immediately before the sale, the capital property must have been used in the business of farming by the vendor, or the vendor's spouse, common-law partner, or child(ren).

There are several reasons why you may want to claim a reserve.

- Old Age Security claw back
- reduction in the non-refundable age tax credit
- loss of the Old Age Supplement and Goods and Services Tax Credit

Maintaining sole proprietor status limits the tax opportunities available to family farmers in Canada, such opportunities as the tax-deferred rollover of farm inventory.

Partnership

A farming partnership is an association of two or more persons in the farming business with shared responsibilities for costs and liabilities, and shared rights to the profits from the farming activities. The income generated from the farm operation is proportionate to the partnership ownership and is taxed at each person's personal marginal tax rate.

Under subsection 70(10) of the ITA, an interest in a family farm partnership of an individual at any time means a partnership interest owned by an individual whereby all or substantially all of the fair market value of the property of the partnership was property used principally in the course of carrying on a farming business in Canada. The property must be used in that farming business by the individual (or by the spouse, child, or parent of the person) and that person must be actively engaged in that farming business on a regular and continuous basis.

A family farm partnership is a common structure for operating a farm in Canada. The major benefit is that inventory forms part of the partnership assets. As a result, therefore, the inventory qualifies for a tax-deferred rollover to a child or to a farm corporation making this structure tax-effective from a succession planning perspective.

Separate and apart from the tax benefits, a family farm partnership is also reflective of how farms operate. It is common for family members to be actively involved in the day-to-day farm operations.

To provide flexibility for future tax-deferred rollovers, farmland is typically not transferred into a partnership. A typical strategy is to allocate specific parcels of farmland to different children to maximize the enhanced capital gains exemption.

It is important to be aware of subsection 69(11) of the ITA. The purpose of this subsection is to ensure that individuals, through a series of transactions, do not transfer land to their children at less than fair market value so that the children receive the benefit of any deduction, including the capital gains exemption. If the child then disposes of the property within three years of the transfer and claims the capital gains exemption at that time, subsection 69(11) of the ITA will deem the first transfer (from parent to child) to have occurred at fair market value. The result is the creation of a capital gain on the original transfer from the parent to the child. The parent will then be taxed on the capital gain.

Corporation

A corporation is a company that is incorporated under either the federal or the provincial government to transact a business. It can be wholly owned by one person or by two or more shareholders.

Unlike a sole proprietor or a partnership, the income earned from the farm operations are taxed in the farming corporation, typically at a rate much lower that the farmer's personal tax rate. The 2014 tax rate for farming corporations in Saskatchewan for example is 13 percent on the first $500,000 of taxable farming income.

The lower tax rates allow for additional funds to retire debt or be reinvested in the farming operations or to save for retirement. Another benefit is that the farming assets become separate from personal assets, an important distinction when undergoing succession planning especially where there are non-farming children involved.

The ITA, under subsection 73(4.1), allows a transfer of an interest in a family farm partnership or a share of capital stock of a family farm corporation to a child on a tax-deferred basis as long as the following conditions under subsection 73(4) of the ITA are met:

a) The child of the taxpayer must be resident in Canada immediately before the transfer, and
b) The property was, immediately before the transfer, a share of the capital stock of a family farm corporation or an interest in a family farm partnership.

In addition, the ITA has extended the definition of "child" to include a spouse of a child. This is important because now the family can multiply the enhanced capital gains exemption.

In order for the shares of a family farm corporation to qualify for the enhanced capital gains exemption, the family farm corporation shares owned must meet the following criteria:

- At trigger date, all or substantially all (90 percent) of the fair market value of the property owned by the corporation was attributable to property used principally in the farming business in which the person, spouse, child, or parent was actively engaged on a regular and continuous basis; and
- At least twenty-four months prior to a trigger date, such as transfer or death, 50 percent or more of the fair market value of the property owned by the corporation was attributable to property used principally in the farming business.

A farmer that owns and farms qualifying farm property or owns an interest in a Family Farm Partnership or shares of a Family Farm Corporation has flexibility in setting up his/her succession plan without incurring any taxation. Be aware, however, that farm inventory can only be transferred on a tax-deferred basis as a consequence of the death of the transferor.

It is important to be aware of the differences between tax deferral and tax savings. If the family farm stays in the family indefinitely and each successive generation farms the property actively, the tax is postponed indefinitely.

It is easy to fall into the trap of the tax deferral of the family farm rollover without taking into consideration the true tax savings that are afforded family farm owners through the enhanced capital gains exemption.

Using the enhanced capital gains exemption wherever possible is typically a sound strategy. It provides for a "bump up" in the adjusted cost base of the farm property as it is transferred from one generation to the next with minimal if any tax consequences, while increasing the adjusted cost base of the farm assets. At the eventual disposition of these assets, the higher adjusted cost base will minimize the capital gain and, therefore, minimize taxes on the farm property sale.

From a tax planning perspective, the benefits available to Lucy and Stan as business owners are also available to shareholders of a qualified family farm corporation.

Farm Succession Planning

As with other small business succession planning, there are several issues, both personal and financial, to decide upon before proceeding with the creation of a succession plan. Each family is unique, so it is important to look at the family dynamics and personal objectives when discussing these important issues. More importantly, don't make tax savings the sole basis of your decisions. It is for your tax advisors to ensure minimal tax leakage.

The following are important considerations when contemplating succession planning:

Ownership and Control

- Are you ready to give up control of the farm operations, or would you like to decrease control as your investment in the farm decreases?
- Which child or children want to be involved in the farm? Are they willing to take over the operations in the near future?

Retirement and Security

- Do you want to maintain ownership until such time that your child or children pay you out?
- Are you willing to guarantee any current farm indebtedness for your child?
- What are your future retirement income needs from the farm?
- What are your commitments to the non-farming children, if any?
- Do you plan to maintain your house on the farm property?
- Can the farm afford to pay you out?

Equal Versus Equitable Treatment of Non-Farming Children

- Are there non-farm assets that the non-farming children will inherit?
- Do you consider these assets an equitable share of your assets?
- Does the farming child have to sell or finance any part of the farm operations to meet the equitable

distribution you have set out?

- Are the farming operations put at risk?
- What is equitable?
- Is it important that the farming child receive the farm intact; that is no financing is required to pay out the non-farming children?
- Is it possible that one or more of the non-farming children might challenge your estate after your death?

Succession Planning and Your Business Structure

Sole Proprietor

As a sole proprietor, you have flexibility in structuring the transfer of your farm business. Consider any of the following:

- **Direct transfer or sale of all your assets.** Remember that inventory does not transfer to your child on a tax-deferred basis. It will be deemed for tax purposes to transfer to your child at fair market value. This will most likely result in unfavourable tax consequences.
- **Transfer of assets to a partnership.** The child will then share net profits of the farming operations.
- **Transfer of assets to a corporation.** The share ownership can be structured so that any future growth of the farming operations will be recognized by your child and the existing value remains with you.

Partnership

The transfer of a partnership interest into a family farm corporation may result in a conversion, on a tax-free basis, of the accrued capital gain in the partnership interest into a shareholder loan owing to the taxpayer from the corporation. The shareholder loan can then be repaid to the shareholder tax-free resulting in the receipt of retained earnings in a non-taxable form. This is an effective distribution of corporate assets because the income is taxed at the small business corporate tax rate (13 percent in Saskatchewan in 2014). This is possible because interests in family farm partnerships qualify for the capital gains deduction. Unfortunately, partnership interests in other types of businesses do not qualify.

Once incorporated, the family farm business now has access to the small business rate. In addition, corporate structures can be implemented to allow for tax-effective retirement and succession planning just like any other small business corporation in Canada.

When deciding on which method is the best in your situation, it is important to acknowledge your needs and review the tax consequences of each option.

Farm Property Dispositions–Are They Always Tax-Free?

I have often heard that farmland qualifies for the capital gains exemption. In most cases, this is a true statement; however, the ITA provides a specific definition for "qualified farm property" eligible for the capital gains exemption. It is defined under subsection 110.6(1) of the ITA in the following way:

- owned by an individual, spouse or common law partner of the individual, or a family farm partnership (defined below) in which the individual, spouse or common-law partner has an interest
- a qualified farm property can include
    * real or immovable property "used principally in the course of carrying on the business of farming" in Canada by
        » the individual
        » a spouse or common-law partner
        » child or parent of the individual
        » a family farm corporation or a family farm partnership in which the individual has an interest
        » beneficiaries of a trust if the individual is a personal trust
    * shares of a family farm corporation
    * interest in a family farm partnership
    * eligible capital property used in the course of carrying on the business of farming in Canada by the individual, a spouse, common-law partner, child or parent of the individual, a family farm

corporation or a family farm partnership owned by the individual, and beneficiaries of a trust if the individual is a personal trust

Specific requirements based on date of acquisition include the following.

If the property was acquired after June 18, 1987

- The farm property must have been owned by the individual for a period of at least twenty-four months immediately preceding the date of sale,
- The gross farming revenue of the individual must have exceeded the income of the operator from all other sources in at least two years while the property was owned by the individual, and
- The property was used by either a family farm corporation or family farm partnership for a period of at least twenty-four months.

If the property was acquired before June 18, 1987

- In the year of disposition, the property is used principally in the business of farming by the individual, or
- The property must have been used principally in the business of farming by the individual for a period of at least five years during which time the property was owned by the individual.

It is important to be aware of the full history of the farm property ownership to ensure that it is "qualified farm property" and eligible for the tax-free rollover to the next generation.

Transfer of a Joint Interest

Where a property is owned by one person and is transferred into "joint tenancy," this may be considered a disposition for income tax purposes. If the property is qualified farm property and is being transferred into joint tenancy with a child, the rollover provisions would be available. In all other cases, the disposition would be required to be reported at fair market value resulting in a potential tax liability to the transferor. Chapter Twelve has a more detailed discussion on Joint Ownership.

The transfer of property into a joint tenancy must be given careful consideration as it can materially change the overall estate. For example, assume that a father transferred land into joint tenancy with his child. The land was qualified farm property at the time of the transfer and the disposition has most likely been reported at the father's adjusted cost base of the land.

An often missed tax-planning opportunity with this type of transfer is the use of the capital gains exemption available to the farmer on the transfer of land from one generation to the next. The father does have the option of reporting proceeds of the transfer at any amount between the adjusted cost base and the fair market value of the asset being transferred into joint tenancy. Ideally, the father would transfer the property at his available capital gains exemption ($800,000 in 2014). The result is that the child now has a bump up in the adjusted cost base of the asset transferred. The downside to the father would be the possibility of paying Alternative Minimum Tax (AMT) for the next several years. AMT can be minimized by the use of the ten-year reserve available to farmers. This would result in only one-tenth of the capital gain inclusion every year for ten years, minimizing if not eliminating AMT.

When the father dies, he is deemed to have disposed of the remaining 50 percent interest directly to his child. If the property is qualified farm property on the date of death, this should not be a problem. However, if the land is no longer considered to be qualified farm property, there will be a deemed disposition at fair market value resulting in an income tax liability arising in the father's terminal return. This liability would be paid out of the estate and would impact the residual beneficiaries. The child would receive this remaining 50 percent interest with a tax cost equal to fair market value.

Family farms have beneficial tax rules for transition to the next generation. It is important that when estate planning for the farm family, consideration be given to the technical tax rules relating to intergenerational rollovers and maximizing the benefits available. Planning techniques should be assessed in light of these special rules and the ability or inability to utilize them. Life insurance can be a useful tool to provide available funding for tax liabilities arising on death or when equalization funds are required for children who are no longer farming the family farm.

In this chapter, we have discussed

- The specific tax benefits that a family farm (or fishing) business has access to
    * lifetime capital gains exemption on the transfer of qualified farm assets,
    * intergenerational tax deferred rollover to a child,
    * the three possible business structures of a family farming business, and
    * joint tenancy of assets.
- The tax rollover rules based on the date of farm ownership: before June 18, 1987 and after June 18, 1987

In Chapter Fifteen–Workbook, you will find additional information

- personal information gathering
- recording your family genome
- will questionnaire
- power of attorney questionnaire
- personal health care directive questionnaire
- risk management

Workbook

The forms and checklists in this chapter are examples only. Full-sized forms can be downloaded from my website: www.integratedwealthtaxstrategies.com

As a business owner reading through this book, this chapter is for you. There are checklists and information gathering tools as well as a more in-depth discussion of certain topics. This chapter is to get your creative juices flowing and help you in taking your first step in your planning process.

- ☐ Personal Information Gathering
- ☐ Recording Your Family Genome
- ☐ Getting Your Business Ready for Sale
- ☐ What Are Your Financial Statements Telling You?
- ☐ The Main Advantages of an Estate Freeze
- ☐ Qualified Small Business Corporation Status
- ☐ Discretionary Family Trusts
- ☐ Checklist - Unanimous Shareholders Agreement
- ☐ Stop-Loss Rules
- ☐ Importance of the Capital Dividend Account
- ☐ Risk Management
- ☐ Individual Pension Plans
- ☐ Will Questionnaire
- ☐ Power of Attorney Questionnaire
- ☐ Personal Health Care Directive Questionnaire
- ☐ United States Residency Status – Is There Need for Concern?

Personal Information Gathering

The purpose of this section is to record your family details all in one place. The importance of United States residency status has heightened over the last several years, so gathering birthplace information will assist in determining whether further action is required. If a family member listed below is a US citizen or green card holder, some of the tax planning opportunities may not be available to them. It is important to get independent professional advice on the potential US tax implications regarding your Canadian tax planning.

Personal Information Gathering	
Your Name	Spouse's Name
Birth Date	Birth Date
Birth Place	Birth Place
Residency for tax purposes	Residency for tax purposes
Marital Status	Date of Marriage

Children			
Name	Birth Date	Birth Place	Occupation

Parents	
Your Parents	Spouse's Parents
Birth Date	Birth Date
Birth Place	Birth Place
Residency for tax purposes	Residency for tax purposes
Marital Status	Marital Status

Personal Goals

When considering your goals, consider them in context to wealth accumulation, retirement, transitioning your business. Consider reviewing Chapter One and the Parke family goals.

Personal Goals
Your Goals
1.
2.
3.
4.
5.
6.
7.
8.
9.
10.
Spouse's Goals
1.
2.
3.
4.
5.
6.
7.
8.
9.
10.

Recording Your Family Genome

Who are the members of your family? Start with your immediate family, then include the relationships that impact your business. See Chapter One – Introduction to the Parke Family for the Parke Family genome as an example.

To draw a family genome use the following symbols: Males – squares; females – circles. Join spouses with a line and include their children. If there is a previous marriage, include that information along with any children from that marriage.

Getting Your Business Ready for Sale

It takes a great deal of effort to prepare a business for sale or partial sale. It is a good time to analyze your business and enhance its value. A strong management team translates to a well-organized business. Not only is this beneficial for attracting a new shareholder, but it is a strong foundation for the future growth of your business.

Taking a good hard look at your business is important. What areas are strong and what areas need improvement? This process is not to criticize past performance, but to look at opportunities for the future.

Focus on sales and profitability. What are your profit margins? When was the last time you increased your prices? Is there an opportunity to do so now? How efficient is the production of the product? Is there opportunity to cut costs without cutting quality?

Establish a good management structure. Ideally, knowledge and talent are not concentrated within only a few individuals. Does the management organization make sense? Document your business decisions and systems.

Highlight the diversity of customers and suppliers. A good balance of customers and suppliers is best. Try to avoid a concentration of either, which could affect the value of your business.

Remove all non-operating assets such as cash and investments. They can be transferred to another company on a tax-deferred basis. This will also assist in the qualification of the $800,000 (2014) capital gains exemption available to shareholders of qualifying shares.

Consider transferring land and equipment to another company. This is mainly for creditor protection, but it also helps to decrease the purchase price of the shares.

Assess your technology. Is your system up to date? Do you have a proper recovery program to minimize losses in case of disruption? Are your systems generating productive management information for you? Do you wish you had more information at your disposal to make effective decisions?

Consider tax issues and tax options. Are the corporate tax filings up to date, including income tax, payroll remittances, GST, and PST? Are you maximizing on all tax credits available to you? Consider Research and Development tax credits, for example.

What Are Your Financial Statements Telling You?

It is important to make the time to read and understand your financial statements. What is your financial information telling you about your business? Ideally, you should review your financial information on a monthly basis, or quarterly, but the reality is that most business owners only see a set of financial statements at year-end.

Although business owners are highly intelligent and great at their businesses, a set of financial statements may look like Greek to them. You are not the only one who feels that way, but it is important that your company has a qualified individual to assist you in understanding what those statements are telling you.

Don't be afraid to ask your accountant what your financial statements say. Ask your accountant to explain, in plain language, not accountant talk, what he/she considers important indicators of your company's financial wellbeing.

Year-end financial statements are made up of a Balance Sheet, Income Statement, and hopefully, a Statement of Cash Flow. Your financial statements are a formal record of the financial activity of your business. Don't drive with your eyes closed. The following three statements provide the company with an accurate picture of the company's financial health.

A **Balance Sheet** provides the business owner with a clear snapshot of what the company liabilities are, the amount he/she has contributed to the company, or contributions from investors, and the value of all assets.

An **Income Statement** provides a clear picture of where the money is earned and where it is being spent and what is left over as profit.

A **Statement of Cash Flow** provides a picture of where the money has entered and exited the business and for what purpose.

With the information contained in the above three statements, you can use the following five formulas to calculate and determine how your company is managing growth.

Gross Profit Margin: The difference between the revenue generated by sales of either a product or service and the cost of making that product or providing the service.

Revenue from sales - Cost of production or service = Gross Profit Margin

Calculating the gross profit margin over several periods—both monthly if information is available and annually over many years—should tell you when cost increases are outpacing your revenue gains.

Operating Margin: The profit that is left after the cost of goods sold, direct wages, and depreciation on the assets used to produce the asset is subtracted from the revenue generated.

Revenue from sales - Cost of goods, wages, and depreciation = Operating Margin (Profit)

Calculating the operating margin shows the full impact of a company's pricing strategy and its operating efficiencies.

For example, an increase in sales may in fact decrease profits. If this is happening you will want to know that information as soon as possible.

This number is an indicator of how effective the company is with expenses and if you were to decrease certain expenses without affecting quality, your profit margins would increase.

Current Ratio:

Current assets ÷ Current liabilities = Current Ratio

The current ratio shows whether the assets convertible to cash within a year will cover your expenses payable within a year. A ratio of less than 1 indicates that you may run short of cash.

Debt to Equity Ratio:

Total liabilities ÷ Shareholder's equity = Debt to Equity Ratio

The debt to equity ratio provides an indication of how much debt the company has taken on compared to what the owners have invested in it. A 2 to 1 ration means that the company has 2 dollars of debt to every 1 dollar of shareholder investment. In other words, the company is taking on twice as much debt as the owners are investing in the company.

Inventory Turnover Ratio: Cost of sales divided by the average inventory value for the period.

Cost of Sales ÷ Average inventory value = Inventory Turnover Ratio

These numbers are derived from the balance sheet and a balance sheet is a snapshot of the company's financial information at one point in time. The average inventory value should take into account both the opening and closing inventory of the period, whether it is monthly, quarterly or annually. The average is calculated by added the opening inventory and the closing inventory of the period and dividing by two. This will provide a more meaningful ratio.

If a company's inventory turnover ratio is 2 to 1, the company's inventory has turned over twice in the reporting period. This could be a favourable ratio depending on your business.

The three components of the financial statement— Balance Sheet, Income Statement, and Statement of Cash Flow—are interrelated. Alone, each statement provides information, but combined these statements provide important information and a more complete picture of the financial health of your company.

The Main Advantages of an Estate Freeze

One of the most important strategies for business succession and estate planning for business owners is an estate freeze. It allows for the transition of the business from one generation to the next on a tax-deferred basis. This is a structure where children are brought into the corporation, typically through a fully discretionary trust without generating adverse tax consequences while at the same time freezing the corporation's value. The future growth of the company is transferred to the children via the trust. The use of the trust allows the owner-manager to retain control of the business and provides the flexibility to determine to whom and when control will be passed on to the next generation in a tax-efficient manner.

It is important to determine why you may want to execute an estate freeze. Would you benefit from a strategy with which you can do the following?

- ☐ cap your capital gains liability on your family business's shares?
- ☐ pass the future growth of the business to your children with no immediate tax?
- ☐ maximize access to the capital gains exemption?
- ☐ structure a stream of dividend income to the retiring shareholder?
- ☐ facilitate a share purchase by an employee or group of employees?

An estate freeze

- allows for flexibility in estate planning through the use of a discretionary family trust.
- allows the business owner to retain the value of his/her company built to date.
- purifies the company's "small business corporation" status.
- facilitates small business expansion planning.
- allows the business owner to remain in control of all corporate assets for as long as he/she wishes.

- allows for income splitting with family members.
- mitigates any capital gains tax on death.
- multiplies the availability of the enhanced capital gains exemption.
- crystallizes capital gains for the enhanced capital gains exemption.
- allows for an orderly, systematic redemption of shares following retirement.
- reduces creditor risk by removing the "growth" value from potential attachment by creditors of the business owner and their family.

Qualified Small Business Corporation Status

The capital gains exemption can be a source of considerable tax savings to a shareholder of a qualified small business corporation. The exemption in 2014 was $800,000 and will be indexed to inflation going forward. An incorporated business has to meet specific criteria to qualify:

- Canadian Controlled Private Corporation—50 percent or more of the shareholders have to be residents of Canada for tax purposes
- meet the twenty-four month holding period
- meet the asset mix requirement—both the 90 percent test and the 50 percent test based on the fair market value of the corporate assets

Does your company meet the criteria or do you have to adopt strategies to ensure that your company will qualify in the future? Have a good look at where your business is today.

- ☐ Are 50 percent or more of the shareholders Canadian residents for tax purposes?
- ☐ Have the shares been held by the shareholder or a person or partnership related to the shareholder for twenty-four consecutive months through to the trigger date, which is a restructuring, sale, transfer, or death.
- ☐ Is 90 percent of the fair market value of the assets currently owned by the corporation used in active business? That is at trigger date.
- ☐ Is 50 percent of the fair market value of the asset owned by the corporation in the twenty-four months prior to the trigger date used in active business?

These rules are restrictive so adopting strategies sooner rather than later is the best plan of action. Typically planning will involve the transfer of non-business assets such as investments and real estate not used for the business into a holding company via a tax-free transfer. This process is termed "purifying the corporation."

Discretionary Family Trust

Trusts are vehicles through which property and assets are managed and administered for the benefit of the trust's beneficiaries. Trusts are created for tax and non-tax reasons such as for spendthrift and incompetent persons.

Although a trust may be tax-motivated, it is usually the protective elements of a trust that become the more important features.

A Discretionary Family Trust is an effective tool in corporate tax and estate planning. It is typically used to allow shareholders to transfer assets to their family without losing control of the asset until such time that they choose. In addition, at their choice, they can slowly ease out of the business. The trust allows for flexibility as to who and when the business owner may want to transfer the control of his/her business.

Trusts can be created in several different ways. Most trusts used in business planning are Inter Vivos trusts, meaning that the trust is created during the lifetime of the settlor. A trust is a legal relationship between three parties:

1. The Settlor—settles a property on a trustee in trust for the benefit of specified beneficiaries
2. The Trustee or Trustees—control the trust and have a fiduciary duty to the beneficiaries of the trust
3. The Beneficiaries—individuals for whom the trust was established

The Settlor

The settlor is the person who settles the trust with an asset that can be almost anything but is typically a $100 bill or a gold or silver coin. Legal title of the property used to settle the trust is transferred to the trustee for the benefit of the beneficiaries. For an Inter Vivos trust, the transfer is during the settlor's lifetime.

The Trustee or Trustees

Trustees are governed by the trust document. It lays out their powers and obligations. At all times, the trustee must act according to the guidelines of "a prudent investor." It is extremely important to assess the person who will take on the role of trustee. To avoid attribution rules and negative tax consequences, the settlor and the trustee should not be the same person.

The Beneficiary or Beneficiaries

The beneficiary is entitled to the use and enjoyment of the assets of the trust. They receive either income or capital, or both, from the trust depending on the terms in the trust deed. A family trust is typically a fully discretionary trust, meaning that the income and/or capital distributions from the trust are fully discretionary and according to the Trustees.

A family trust is usually created in conjunction with an estate freeze to provide a tax efficient way to maximize the capital gains exemption and to income split with family members without their having direct ownership of the company.

The advantages of a family trust include these:

- maximum flexibility and discretion in so far as who will receive what and when
- complete retention of control by the business owner at all times
- protection against potential claims by creditors of the business owner and their family, with respect to the assets held in the trust. The trust may protect against possible claims by future spouses of their children pursuant to matrimonial property proceedings. Division of property rules fall under the jurisdiction of provincial matrimonial laws. It is imperative that legal counsel is obtained, specific to your province of residence, to determine how the matrimonial laws impact fully discretionary trusts.
- the ability at any point in the future to transfer assets directly to beneficiaries of the trust without any adverse income tax implications or other significant costs
- the highest degree of confidentiality
- the ability to benefit present children and future grandchildren
- multiplication of the family's access to the $800,000 (2014) enhanced capital gains exemption. Assuming future growth in value, this can eliminate the tax liability by a factor of $800,000 for each adult beneficiary.

For tax planning purposes, we would also recommend that the income and capital interests of any minor children not vest until they reach the age of majority and no income or capital be paid to them until that time. This should be stated in the trust documents.

In addition, it is important to note that under the current law, living trusts are deemed to dispose of their capital property every twenty-one years and this important date should be noted and a provision included in the trust documents allowing the trustees to transfer any or all of the assets of the trust to beneficiaries prior to expiration of the said twenty-one-year period. If appropriately structured, this transfer can occur on a tax-deferred basis.

Checklist—Unanimous Shareholder Agreement

Like any contract, the provisions in a shareholder agreement are limited only by the imagination and skill of the drafters. Consequently, it is impossible to provide an exhaustive list of all possible issues and tax consequences that might arise in any given shareholder agreement. The checklists/forms provided here include a number of the common issues to consider when drafting a thorough buy-sell agreement. These are designed to get your creative juices flowing.

- ☐ General Information
- ☐ Corporate Structure
- ☐ Shareholder Information
- ☐ Triggering Events
- ☐ Buy-Sell Arrangement for Triggering Events
- ☐ Other Considerations

This exercise does not replace the proper creation of a shareholders' agreement or the need for a lawyer to ensure the shareholders' intent and wishes are achieved through the agreement. The information that you gather will be the basis upon which your agreement will be drafted and should be given to your lawyer for use in preparing the shareholder agreement.

General Information		
Legal name of business		
Incorporation date		
Doing business as		
Address		
Phone number		
Fax number		
Website address		
Further online presence		
Nature of business		
Corporate year-end		
Restructure date		
Preferred shares redemption value		
Business Structure		
☐ Sole Proprietor	☐ Partnership	☐ Incorporation
Date of incorporation/purchase/start		
Value of corporation		
At inception		
Current estimate		
Restrictions on share transfers		

Corporate Structure

What is the corporate structure of your business and of other related corporations, businesses, and/or trusts?

Draw a full picture and description of the corporate structure. For ease of understanding, use the following symbols: Corporations – squares; individuals – circles; partnerships – ovals; and trusts – triangles. Chapter Four has an example of a corporate structure for your reference.

Shareholder Information

Class of Share:			Voting or Non-Voting:		
Shareholder Name	# of Shares	%	Redemption Value	Tax Residence	Country of Birth

Class of Share:			Voting or Non-Voting		
Shareholder Name	# of Shares	%	Redemption Value	Tax Residence	Country of Birth

Class of Share:			Voting or Non-Voting		
Shareholder Name	# of Shares	%	Redemption Value	Tax Residence	Country of Birth

Triggering Events

	Yes	No
Death of a shareholder		
Long-term disability		
Critical Illness		
Retirement from business		
Marital breakdown		
Resignation		
Termination		
Bankruptcy of the shareholder		
Desire to sell		

Buy-Sell Arrangement for Triggering Events

	Shotgun	Mandatory	Right of First Refusal	Option Put-Call
Death of a shareholder				
Long-term disability				
Critical Illness				
Retirement from business				
Marital breakdown				
Resignation				
Termination				
Bankruptcy of the shareholder				
Desire to sell				

Definitions for the triggering events above:

Shotgun: In the case of disagreement, there are clauses that ensure that one of the parties to the disagreement will be removed as a shareholder. Often, a shotgun clause will be included in the agreement to address this situation.

Mandatory: In the case of death, it is mandatory for the buy-sell agreement to trigger either a redemption of shares or sale of shares to surviving shareholders.

Right of First Refusal: This allows the other shareholder the first option to acquire the shares.

Option Put-Call: A "put" right is the right of a surviving spouse (or spousal trust) to require a purchase of the estates shares by either the surviving shareholders, the corporation, or a combination of the shareholders and the corporation in the proportions determined by the spouse or spousal trust.

A "call" right is the option to purchase or to cause the corporation to purchase the shares held by a spouse or spousal trust. This is exercised when the "put" right has not been exercised by the spouse or spousal trust.

Other Considerations

Generally speaking, the USA should contain certain elements.

- ☐ intent of the agreement to provide overall guidance of the terms and conditions set out in the agreement
- ☐ list of triggering events and specific definitions relating to each event to ensure clarification
- ☐ valuation method or party who will provide the valuation with a mechanism for arbitration should the need arise
- ☐ clear definition of buy-sell funding
- ☐ availability and use of the general rate income pool (GRIP) for eligible dividends

Upon the death of a shareholder, consider the following:

- ☐ rollover of shares to a spouse. Ensure this clause ties into the shareholder's will.
- ☐ shares issued prior to April 26, 1995. Consider the effect of the agreement to preserve grandfathering privileges.
- ☐ funding by life insurance prior to April 26, 1995. Consider the effect of the agreement to preserve grandfathering privileges.
- ☐ Do the corporate shares qualify for the capital gains exemption?
- ☐ What is the available capital gains exemption per shareholder?

Upon disability or critical illness, consider the following:

☐ Is a critical illness an immediate triggering event? If not, when does a critical illness become a triggering event?

☐ Will the disabled shareholder continue to own shares of the company during his/her period of disability?

☐ If shares will be owned, will the disabled shareholder continue to benefit from the further growth of the company or will the shareholder's interest be frozen in the value of preferred shares up to the time of disability?

☐ How will the disabled shareholder fund the cost of living after the disability? How much will the shareholder need?

☐ Are the shareholders able to purchase either or both disability and critical illness insurance to help fund the future living costs?

☐ Will the value of the disabled shareholder's shares be sufficient to allow the shareholder to earn enough income from the capital to meet the cost of living and providing for his/her family?

☐ If there is a shortfall in the value of shares, will the company fund a portion of the costs through payment of dividends to the disabled shareholder? If so, for how long?

☐ Will there be sufficient funds in the estate to provide for the shareholder's family after his/her death?

☐ Will the company continue to pay the life insurance premiums for the disabled shareholder? Will their family be entitled to the proceeds upon the death of the shareholder?

☐ If the disabled shareholder holds voting shares, who will vote the shares? The USA should consider this possibility and provide for a power of attorney to deal with the corporate property.

Upon marital breakdown consider the following:

☐ The corporate shares may be subject to division of property rules under provincial matrimonial law.
☐ The corporation may have the addition of an unwanted shareholder, the former spouse of the divorcing shareholder. If the result is not an additional shareholder, at minimum there is the potential for considerable debt to the divorcing shareholder to buy out his/her former spouse.
☐ Provisions may be added to the USA to address this situation. Does the divorcing shareholder have the funding available to buy out his/her spouse if shares are awarded under the terms of the division of assets? If not, consider a provision that would allow the remaining shareholders the entitlement to buy out the divorcing shareholder's shares subject to the division of assets allocated to the former spouse.

Stop-Loss Rules

In 1995, the federal government implemented the Stop Loss Rules. They are intended to reduce a taxpayer's loss on the sale of his/her shares by the amount of tax-free dividends received on those shares.

The Stop Loss Rules are based on three very important tax rules:

1. At date of death, a taxpayer is deemed to have disposed of all of his/her assets at fair market value.
2. Proceeds on a corporate share redemption are equal to the Paid Up Capital (PUC) of the share; any proceeds over the PUC is deemed by Canada Revenue Agency to be a dividend. The dividend can be either a Capital Dividend (tax-free) or a taxable dividend.
3. The estate of a deceased taxpayer can carry a loss back to the deceased's terminal tax return if the disposition of the corporate shares are made within one year of death.

The following example illustrates the impact of the stop-loss rules upon the death of a shareholder of a Canadian Controlled Private Corporation. The example makes these assumptions:

1. Jonathan is a widower and sole shareholder of his company, Widget Inc.
2. The FMV of Widget Inc. at the time of Jonathan's death is $1 Million.
3. The Adjusted Cost Base (ACB) and the PUC of Jonathan's shares is $10,000.
4. Because Jonathan is a widower, no spousal rollover is available.

Tax Implications Pre Stop Loss Rules 1995		
	Jonathan's Terminal Tax Return	Estate's Tax Return
FMV/Proceeds Received: Widget Inc. shares	$1,000,000	$1,000,000
Less: Deemed Dividend (Proceeds - PUC)	$990,000	($990,000)*
Adjusted Proceeds for tax purposes	$1,000,000	$10,000
Capital Gain (Jonathan)/ Capital Loss (Estate)	$990,000	($990,000)
Loss Carry back to Jonathan from Estate**	($990,000)	-
Adjusted Capital Gain	$0	-
Taxes Payable	Nil	Nil

*Rule 2 above **Rule 3 below

Tax Implications Post Stop Loss Rules - Jonathan's Terminal Tax Return	
Fair Market Value of Widget Inc. shares	$1,000,000
Adjusted Cost Base of Widget Inc. shares	$10,000
Capital Gain	$990,000
Loss Carry Back from Estate (50% stop loss rule)	($495,000)
Taxable Capital Gain	$495,000
Taxes Payable (assume 45% tax rate)	$222,750

Tax Implications Post Stop Loss Rules - Estate's Tax Return	
Proceeds of Widget Inc. shares	$1,000,000
Deemed Dividend (Rule 2 above)	($990,000)*
Adjusted Proceeds	$10,000
Adjusted Cost Base of Shares to the Estate	($1,000,000)
Capital Loss to the Estate	($990,000)
Adjusted Loss (Stop Loss Rules: 50% of Capital dividend paid to Estate)**	$495,000
Revised Capital Loss carried back to Jonathan's Terminal Return	($495,000)
Taxable Dividend to Estate/ Taxes Payable	Nil
*Proceeds less Paid Up Capital	$990,000
Capital Dividend paid to Estate (tax-free)	$990,000**

To summarize, the stop-loss rules limit an estate's ability to carry back losses to the deceased's terminal tax return when the estate has received capital dividends on the deceased's share redemption. More specifically, where the estate has received capital dividends on the share that exceed one half of the deceased's gain on death, the loss available for carry back will be reduced by the amount of the excess. The stop-loss rules in subsection 112(3.2) do not apply if the shares are grandfathered. Essentially the share sale must occur pursuant to an agreement in writing made before April 27, 1995 or the corporation must have been a beneficiary of a life insurance policy on the life of the individual on April 26, 1995 and a main purpose of the policy was to fund the share redemption. Where the grandfathering rules do not apply, certain planning techniques may be utilized.

The Importance of The Capital Dividend Account

The Capital Dividend Account is a fundamental tax-planning tool for private Canadian corporations and their shareholders; public corporations do not qualify for this treatment.

Taxation in Canada is based on the fundamental tax principle of integration. Under this principal for example, individuals are taxed on 50 percent of a realized capital gain, the other 50 percent is theirs tax-free. Corporations are afforded the same tax treatment, which is, 50 percent of the realized capital gain is taxed in the corporation; the other 50 percent is a tax-free receipt. The issue, therefore, is how do shareholders receive the tax-free portion of the capital gain realized by the corporation? The mechanism set out by Canada Revenue Agency is the capital dividend account.

The capital dividend account is a notional account that is created to track certain tax-free receipts of a private corporation that may be distributed as tax-free capital dividends to its shareholders.

The capital dividend account is populated with:

- the excess of the non-taxable portion of capital gains over the non-deductible portion of capital losses incurred by the corporation (after 1971)
- capital dividends received from other corporations
- untaxed portion of gains on eligible capital property
- the life insurance proceeds net of the policy's adjusted cost basis immediately before the time of death
- the non-taxable portion of capital gains distributed by a trust to the corporation in respect of capital gains of the trust

Risk Management

Life is unpredictable. Unforeseen events can sometimes wreak havoc on the best-laid plans. Managing risk is a major element of your financial plan. There are two areas of risk management: 1) insurable risks, such as your life and home; and 2) investment risk, such as the rate of return on your investments.

Insurance products are excellent tools to help deal with uncertainties and protect your lifestyle and your family. It is important, however, to correctly match the right insurance products with your needs.

Your stage in life will determine your risk-management needs. A single individual's needs will be different from the needs of a married couple with a young family or of a couple reaching retirement.

A young family's main concern is providing for the spouse and child or children. Their focus is on these aspects:

- protecting the ability to earn an income
- covering debts in an emergency
- protecting the family
- investing tax efficiently
- planning for retirement

The types of risk coverage the young family need are as follows:

- life insurance for income replacement
- life insurance for mortgage debt replacement
- long-term disability insurance
- critical illness insurance
- health and travel insurance

A family with teenage or older children might be concerned with wealth building for retirement and estate planning—these are the "saving" years. Their focus is on the following:

- protecting the ability to earn an income
- protecting the family
- investing tax efficiently
- planning for retirement
- protecting retirement assets
- creating tax efficient retirement income

The types of risk coverage they need are as follows:

- life insurance for income replacement or debt
- life insurance for wealth management
- long-term disability insurance
- critical illness insurance
- health and travel insurance

A family that is entering the retirement stage—with their children grown—might be concerned with wealth preservation and wealth transfer. Their focus is on the following:

- tax efficient investing
- efficient estate planning
- wealth protection
- efficient retirement income
- protect oneself when no longer able to do so

The types of risk coverage a couple going into retirement may need are as follows:

- life insurance for wealth management
- critical illness insurance
- independent living insurance
- health and travel insurance
- annuities
- segregated funds

Definitions of these risk-management tools :

Term life insurance: Life insurance coverage for a specified term, such as ten-year coverage. Term life insurance is typically used for mortgage insurance or corporate debt or wage replacement for a family. Term insurance is like renting an insurance policy. The cost of the policy in the first ten years is affordable; however, the cost to renew the insurance for the next ten years typically increases substantially, especially as you age. If you are no longer insurable, you are still insured as long as the premiums are paid.

Permanent life insurance: Life insurance coverage that remains in effect for the lifetime of the insured.

- Whole life insurance: Includes a tax-deferred savings component managed by the insurance company. It is designed as a long-term financial planning vehicle. Generally, there are guaranteed minimum cash surrender values. These policies can be participating policies, which means that the policy earns income based on the insurance company's payout. These dividends can be paid out of the policy or can be reinvested into the policy to purchase "paid up additions." The credit earned each year is reinvested to purchase a single premium insurance amount. Over time, the amount purchased will increase the cash surrender value and will itself generate annual credits.

- Universal life insurance: Includes a tax-deferred investment component that is controlled by the life insurance policy owner. It is designed as a long-term financial planning vehicle, combining both cash accumulation and insurance coverage.
- Whole life and universal life insurance policies are typically referred to as tax-sheltered investment accounts.
- Term to 100 insurance: this does not include an investment component but provides coverage to age 100. Generally all the benefits and costs associated with a Term to 100 do not change; there is a level death benefit, meaning it does not increase over time and the premiums are also level and paid until the age of 100. If the insured lives beyond the age of 100, the life insurance stays in force and is payable upon death.

Long-term Disability Insurance: Insurance coverage that provides you with income in the event that you become totally disabled due to illness or injury.

Critical Illness Insurance: Insurance coverage that provides a tax-free lump-sum cash payment upon diagnosis of a range of covered critical illnesses such as heart attack, cancer, and stroke.

Independent Living Insurance: Insurance coverage that pays the cost of your care over a long period of time while you are no longer able to perform two or more activities of daily living.

Health and Travel Insurance: Insurance coverage that is a lifelong need to cover medical expenses not covered by your provincial plan, such as dental and prescriptions. Travel insurance is to cover costs while you are out of the country.

The following two products are offered by insurance companies but they do not meet the traditional insurance definition:

Annuities: The right to receive a fixed annual amount for life or for a certain number of years. The payments can start immediately or they can be deferred to start at a specified time in the future. Non-prescribed annuities have a very favourable tax treatment. Depending on the age of the annuitant, the payment received from a non-prescribed annuity can be two-thirds return of capital and one-third taxable.

Segregated Funds: A segregated fund is a pool of assets held by the insurance company to cover its liability for the corresponding insurance contract. Segregated funds can participate in both public and private investment offerings. They also provide a minimum of 75 percent guaranteed on the capital invested in the fund if the contract is held until maturity or upon the death of the life insured.

Individual Pension Plans

Individual Pension Plans (IPPs) are becoming a popular option for business owners and professionals whose existing retirement savings are inadequate for their retirement needs.

IPPs are alternative retirement savings vehicles. They are defined benefit pension plans, recognized as Registered Pension Plans (RPPs) by the Canada Revenue Agency. IPPs are designed to provide more pension benefits than are available from traditional vehicles such as RRSPs.

IPPs can only be established by corporations, not by individuals themselves. IPP plan holders must be Canadian residents and must pay Canadian income tax and earn a salary from the sponsoring company. The plans are often set up for business owners who would like to make higher contributions to a retirement plan than is currently permitted by the rules governing RRSPs, and who are looking for corporate tax deductions. The investments for IPPs are those eligible for use in a defined benefit pension plan, including stocks, investment funds, or Guaranteed Interest Certificates (GICs), as long as no single equity position represents more than 10 percent of the total book value of the plan.

The plans are attractive due to their higher tax-deductible contribution limits, available tax-deductible contributions for past service, and protection from creditors.

Past service contributions are one of the major advantages offered by IPPs. It is the ability to make contributions in respect of past service to the corporation. Effectively, the shareholder can start an IPP once the corporation is generating adequate cash flow; yet get past service credits from when he/she first incorporated the business. In order to receive past service contributions, however, the shareholder must have received salary in the years in which he/she is claiming the past service contribution. Dividend income does not qualify for IPP calculations.

Newly incorporated businesses are prohibited from offering past-service contributions, even if the employee in question performed identical services to the employer before the incorporation took place.

If the company is making past service contributions on behalf of the shareholder, a Past Service Pension Adjustment (PSPA) has to be made. This calculation is done by a qualified actuary. In effect, it is not possible to have the ability to contribute 100 percent to both an RRSP and an IPP. That would be double dipping. The adjustment is based on the years being claimed for past service contributions. In order to fund past service contributions, individuals are required to transfer an amount equal to the PSPA from their personal RRSPs to the IPP, thereby eliminating the double dipping contributions. The PSPA is calculated by an actuary.

As long as an IPP has been established in good faith by the employer and the employee, the assets will be protected from creditors, making the IPP an attractive alternative for small business owners and professionals.

All IPP calculations must follow the guidelines established by CRA. The guidelines are based on the age of sixty-five as the target retirement age; however, if an IPP holder retires earlier, he/she has the option of making a contribution to "top up" the plan's assets. This top up provides enhanced retirement benefits. These additional top-up contributions are also tax deductible to the corporation.

Another top-up feature of IPPs is when the market takes a downturn. In an RRSP, if the market takes a downturn, any loss affects the ultimate retirement income generated by the RRSP. It could take years, if ever, for the RRSP to recover. In a market downturn, an IPP allows for a top up of the loss of market value. The additional contributions to make up the downturn are tax deductible to the corporation.

All IPP contributions, set-up fees, and maintenance fees made by a corporation on behalf of the employee/shareholder are fully tax deductible to the corporation and treated as a non-taxable benefit to the employee. Interest on funds borrowed by the corporation to top up or fund IPPs are also fully tax deductible by the contributing company. RRSP loans do not have this benefit.

IPPs are subject to both pension and tax legislation and as such must meet the rules and regulations governing them. There are, therefore, initial costs to setting up an IPP as well as annual compliance costs. Every three years an actuarial valuation is required to ensure there are enough funds in the plan. Annual IPP contributions are based on the actuary's report.

The pension income for the plan holder is calculated according to a formula based on a number of factors, such as years of service and salary levels. As a defined benefit plan, an IPP does not have a predetermined contribution limit (such as exists with RRSPs). A defined benefit plan, as the name suggests, defines a benefit that will be paid out to the employee at retirement. In contrast, an RRSP or Defined Contribution Plan will provide a pension benefit equal to what is available in the plan at retirement.

At retirement, the IPP member owns any actuarial

surplus. It may be used to upgrade pension benefits or the plan holder may pass it on to a spouse, heirs, or the estate.

The IPP provides guaranteed lifetime income to the plan holder and upon their death, to their spouse. Eligible spouses receive 66.7 percent of pension in the event of death of the plan member. The plan holder has the option to change many of the pension benefits at retirement. One of the common changes is an upgrade of the spousal benefit to 100 percent of the plan member's pension.

Typically, on the death of the second spouse, registered assets create a tax liability. Any remaining registered assets are fully taxable on the date-of-death tax return of the second spouse. Depending on the balance in the registered assets, as much as 50 percent of the value can be eroded due to taxes. An IPP, although considered a registered asset, has a great option for family businesses. If the business is continuing after the parent retires, and a family member (usually a son or daughter) is taking over the business, they can be added as a member of the existing IPP plan. By leaving the plan intact, any assets not used to provide benefits to the retired parents will remain in the IPP and are transferred to the second generation without triggering tax.

The sponsoring company has 120 days after their year-end to contribute to an IPP and claim a deduction for that taxation year. For example, if your company has a corporate year-end of July 31, 2015, they will have until November 28, 2015 to make their 2015 contributions. This allows for IPP planning well after the taxation year, while also providing tax relief for the previous taxation year.

Most small businesses are sold to family members or partners. The proceeds from these types of asset sales are treated as taxable income. By setting up an IPP using terminal funding, a deduction can be created against this income minimizing the tax effect of the business sale.

One of the most attractive features is the possibility of terminal funding. While CRA restricts the benefits that can be pre-funded, at retirement, an IPP can be amended to provide the most generous terms possible.

Some of these terms include full consumer price indexing, early retirement pension with no reduction, and/or bridge benefits. A business owner has the option of enhancing his/her IPP benefits if the funding permits.

If a business owner chooses to terminate the IPP upon retirement rather than keeping the IPP active, his/her options are as follows:

- an annuity purchased from an insurance company
- a lump sum commuted value of accrued pension benefits, transferred to a locked-in RRSP or locked-in RRIF/LIF up to a maximum amount prescribed by Income Tax Regulations. IPP assets in excess of the maximum transfer limit will be taxed as income to the member and applicable withholding taxes will apply.

In the case of a deficit, the company will have the option whether to fund the IPP or not. If the employer does not choose to fund the deficit, and at the point of retirement there is still a deficit in the plan this will not have an effect on the pension paid. This will only mean that the pension funds will run out sooner.

In the case of excess surplus at the time of the Periodic Valuation Report:

- If the surplus is approximately twice the amount of the current service contribution for that current year, no contribution can be made to the plan until the level of surplus is below the excess surplus and this surplus will be used in place of current service contributions, or
- If the surplus is less than twice the amount of the current service contribution, then the plan sponsor can go ahead and fund the current service if they wish (again, funding is not mandatory).

As stated earlier, all actuarial calculations are based on the following assumptions as outlined in the Income Tax Regulations:

- Rate of Return pre/post retirement: 7.5%
- Inflation rate pre-retirement: 5.5%
- Inflation rate post-retirement: 4.0%
- Retirement age: 65

Form of pension received at retirement:

- joint and last survivor
- reducing to 66.7 percent upon annuitant's death
- five year guarantee

To ensure that the IPP is correctly administered and that the rules and regulations are adhered to, CRA requires either a corporate trustee (financial institution) or three individual trustees. There is no requirement for one of the trustees to be independent, meaning that all three trustees could be family members or shareholders of the company. The only requirement is that the trustees must be residents of Canada.

Will Questionnaire

In order to prepare a Will, it is important to gather information about yourself and how you would like your assets distributed upon your death. The following is meant to get your creative juices flowing and to get you started on the process of completing your will. The following is not a replacement for a will, but will give you a systematic approach to preparing for a meeting with your lawyer who will prepare a will according to your wishes.

Will Questionnaire						
Full Legal Name						
Spouse's Legal Name						
Marital Status	Married		Common-Law	Separated		Divorced
Executor/Executrix	Legal Name			Relation		City of Residence
Second choice						
Third choice						

Children

Legal Name	Address	Date of Birth	Age	Country of Birth

Guardian for Child(ren)

	Legal Name	Relation	City of Residence
First choice			
Second choice			
Third choice			
Child who is mentally of physically Impaired	Yes	No	Added Resources

Other

Disposition of Remains	Organ Donation	Cremation	Burial	Research	Other

Assets Held Within Your Province of Residence				
Description	Value	Jointly Held	With Whom	Beneficiary
Real estate				
RRSP				
TFSA				
Life Insurance				

Assets Held Outside Your Province of Residence				
Description	Value	Jointly Held	With Whom	Beneficiary
Real estate				
Stocks				
Family Cottage				

Who Is to Receive the Balance of the Estate		
Asset Description	Name	Address

When determining who will receive the benefits of your will, consider the following:

- If married, the normal course is that your estate transfers to your spouse. If this is not your wish, how would you like your estate distributed?
- If your spouse dies before you, or you are presently separated or divorced, or your spouse is already deceased and you have children, who gets the rest of your estate? Consider the following options:
  * divided into as many equal shares as you have children alive at your death
  * if the deceased child has children, divided equally among his/her children
  * if to be divided among children and other named beneficiaries, provide name, address, and details of the proportion and to whom your estate should be distributed

Other considerations:

- At what age(s) should any minors receive their share of the estate? For example, consider 25 percent distribution at age twenty-five; the balance of the estate at age thirty-five.
- If you have any special gifts of property that you wish to transfer to relatives, friends, charities, religious organizations, educational organizations, etc., then provide the name of the person/organization and their address; describe the property in detail and provide its location (e.g., specific cash gift, family heirlooms, antiques, jewellery held in the bank safe deposit box).

Power of Attorney Questionnaire

To prepare a Power of Attorney, you need the following information. This is not intended to replace a properly drafted Power of Attorney, but to get your juices flowing and information gathered for your meeting with the lawyer who will draw up the Power of Attorney document.

An "attorney" in this instance does not refer to a lawyer. It is someone you name to act on your behalf, to make decisions respecting your financial affairs.

Power of Attorney				
Your Legal Name				
Power of Attorney	Legal Name		Relation	City of Residence
First Choice				
Second Choice				
Third Choice				
When should Power of Attorney take effect			Immediately	When Incapacitated
Authority to make incapacity decision		Attorney	Doctor	Family Member
Name				
Name				
Name				
Any restrictions on Attorney's authority		Yes	No	Description

Personal Health Care Directive Questionnaire

To prepare a personal health care directive, you need the following information. This is not intended to replace a properly drafted personal health care directive, but to get your juices flowing and information gathered for your meeting with the lawyer who will draw up the personal health care directive according to your wishes.

Personal Health Care Directive Questionnaire					
Your Legal Name					
Maiden Name	Address		City/Province	Phone Number	
Marital Status	Married	Common-Law	Separated	Divorced	

Children

Legal Name	Address	City/Country	Date of Birth	Age

Personal Health Care Directive Agent

Legal Name	Address	Relationship	Home Phone	Work Phone	Cell

Alternate Agent

Personal Medical Information			
Doctor's Name			
Specialization			
Address	City	Phone Number	Emergency Number
Doctor's Name			
Specialization			
Address	City	Phone Number	Emergency Number
Doctor's Name			
Specialization			
Address	City	Phone Number	Emergency Number

Current Medications		
Medication	Doctor	Dose

Medication Allergies	
Medication	Medication

Personal Health Care Guidelines		
My agent must instruct my health care providers based on the following guidelines		
Description	Yes	No
I do not wish my life to be prolonged by artificial means when I am in a coma, persisted vegetative state or have irreversible brain damage or an irreversible brain disease and, in the opinion of my physician and other consultants, have no known hope of regaining awareness and higher mental functions, no matter what is done		
I wish to be kept comfortable and free from pain. This means that I may be given pain mediation even though it may dull consciousness and indirectly shorten my life.		
I wish to live independently for as long as possible and to remain independent in my own accommodations for as long as my Agent deems advisable, having regard to all of the circumstances, including my physical and mental well being, the size of my estate and spouse's (if applicable) income requirements.		
It is my wish that at the appropriate time as determined by my Agent, my Agent permit any of my physical organs/tissues that are suitable for transplant purposes to be so used. This statement shall constitute a consent to donate my body for transplant and/or research.		
Other		

United States Residency Status—Is There Need For Concern?

There are many differences between the tax laws governing United States of America (US) and Canada. Here are some of the most important distinctions:

- Canadian citizens are taxed based on their residency status. If they have emigrated from Canada, Canadian citizens are taxed in Canada only on income earned in Canada.
- US citizens, green card holders and deemed residents for tax purposes are taxed on their worldwide income regardless of where they reside. If a US citizen lives outside the US, they are still required to file an annual US tax return reporting their worldwide income for the year.
- Canada does not have an estate tax.
- US has an estate tax.

The process of determining your US citizenship status is arduous and complicated. Consider the following table to determine whether or not to seek professional advice from a US tax expert to conclude whether or not you are a US Citizen.

United States Citizenship		
1	Born in the US	US Citizen
2	Born in Canada to two US Citizens	US Citizen
3	Born in Canada to one US Citizen	US Citizen if:
	Born on or after November 14, 1986: a) US Parent resided in the US for five years b) Two years of which were after that US parent's 14th birthday	
	Born before November 14, 1986: a) US Parent resided in the US for ten years b) Five years of which were after that US parent's 14th birthday	
4	US Green Card Holders	US Citizen
Termination of income tax and reporting requirements not effective until Form 8854 filed		

If you are a US citizen, tax planning becomes more difficult as some tax regimes in Canada are not mirrored in the US. This planning is beyond the scope of this book and will not be discussed herein.

Deemed residency in the US can also be an issue for "Canadian Snowbirds." Snowbirds are Canadians who spend the winter months in a warm state such as California, Florida, or Arizona. It is important that they are aware of the 183-day rule. Many assume that the 183-day rule means that they can be in the US for 182 days or less per year and be safe for tax purposes. That is not correct. The following table illustrates the actual calculation:

	183 Day Rule Calculation - Accidental US Residents	
A	All days of current year	182
B	1/3 days of previous year	60
C	1/6 days of second previous year	30
	A +B + C	272
and	Current year stayed 31 days or more	Yes
	Met the Substantive Presence Test: Deemed US resident for tax purposes	

This calculation shows that if a Canadian resident spends 182 days per year, over a three-year period, they will have exceeded the 183-day rule and deemed to be resident of the US with all of the tax rules that go with that status. You are required to file an annual tax return reporting your worldwide income. The Canada-US tax treaty does allow for foreign tax credits in one country so taxes payable may be minimal. In addition, you are subject to the US estate tax regime.

There is an out clause if you meet the Substantive Presence Test per the calculations above. You will not be deemed a US resident for tax purposes if you meet the following conditions:

- You were present in the US less than 182 days during the year.
- You established that during the year you had a tax home in a foreign country for example – Canada.
- You established that during the year you had a closer connection to one foreign country, Canada, than to the US.
- You file the Internal Revenue Service ("IRS") Form 8840 to claim the closer connection to a foreign country exception to the Substantial Presence Test.
- You file Form 8840 by June 15th of the year following the Substantive Presence Test trigger.

The actual number of days, if maintained for three consecutive years, to avoid triggering the Substantial Presence Test is 122 days. This is 60 days less per year than the misconceived 183-day rule.

Author Biography

With years of experience advising clients and financial advisors on succession, tax, and estate planning solutions for business owners and high net worth individuals, Marilyn deRooy-Pearson brings a wealth of knowledge and technical expertise to her book about an integrated approach to effective structure, financial, and estate planning.

As a public speaker, she has spoken across Canada to business owners and their trusted advisors, educating them on tax structures and the tax benefits specifically available to business owners and the importance of integrating family, business, and shareholder wishes. While working at Empire Life, Marilyn was instrumental in creating a financial education series for women—P.I.N.K.—Protection Investment and Need for Knowledge—and has delivered these seminars across Canada, from Victoria to Newfoundland. Marilyn also created BOSS – Business Owners Succession Series, specifically geared to educating financial advisors on succession planning for the business owner in Canada.

After graduating from the University of Alberta with a Bachelor of Commerce, Marilyn obtained her Chartered Accountant designation and completed her specialization in tax. Marilyn had her own accounting practice specializing in Owner Managed Businesses, worked in the tax group of Ernst & Young, and then joined Empire Life as their tax and estate-planning specialist for Western Canada. As the need for integrating tax planning and personal financial needs became increasingly important for business owners, Marilyn obtained her Certified Financial Planner (CFP), Chartered Life Underwriter (CLU), and Registered Trust and Estate Practitioner (TEP) designations.

Today Marilyn is the founding principal of Integrated Wealth & Tax Strategies Inc. Their focus is an integrated personalized approach to financial, tax and estate planning for business owners and their families, leveraging tax laws specific to the business owner in Canada.

Further Information About the Author:

Marilyn deRooy-Pearson is the owner and founder of Integrated Wealth & Tax Strategies Inc., and since 2006, she has been an active speaker at national financial events and various seminars across Western Canada. As a Chartered Accountant specializing in tax and a Certified Financial Planner, Chartered Life Underwriter and a Trust and Estate Practitioner, Marilyn brings a wealth of knowledge and technical expertise to such topics as corporate planning, retirement options, and estate planning for business owners and their families. Marilyn is also a member of the Chartered Professional Accountants of British Columbia, the Canadian Tax Foundation, Advocis, Independent Financial Brokers of Canada (IFB) and the Conference of Advanced Life Underwriting (CALU). Speaking appearances include:

- Advocis Seminars—The Financial Advisors Association of Canada, 2007 – 2014
- Advocis Banff School, Banff, Alberta, 2008
- EduVacation at the Advocis Okanagan School, Kelowna, British Columbia, 2014
- IFB—Independent Financial Brokers of Canada, Spring and Fall Summits 2009, 2013, 2014, 2015
- Insight Annual Conferences, Whistler 2011 – 2013, Banff 2014
- Chartered Professional Accountants of BC— Wealth Management Series 2015

To learn more about Marilyn, please visit her LinkedIn profile or contact her directly at: marilyn@integratedwealthtaxstrategies.com.

Twitter: @LeverageTaxLaws
Facebook: Paying Too Much Tax
Website: www.integratedwealthtaxstrategies.com

If you want to get on the path to becoming a published author with Influence Publishing please go to www.InfluencePublishing.com

Inspiring books that influence change

More information on our other titles and how to submit your own proposal can be found at www.InfluencePublishing.com

CPSIA information can be obtained at www.ICGtesting.com
Printed in the USA
LVOW04s0414130515

438245LV00021B/303/P